MARRIAGE IN HEAVEN
by
RONALD FRASER

Author of
"The Flying Draper," "Landscape with Figures,"
"Flower Phantoms," "The Vista," "Rose Anstey"

New York
Charles Scribner's Sons
1933

Printing Statement:

Due to the very old age and scarcity of this book,
many of the pages may be hard to read due to the
blurring of the original text, possible missing pages,
missing text and other issues beyond our control.

Because this is such an important and rare work, we
believe it is best to reproduce this book regardless of
its original condition.

Thank you for your understanding.

MARRIAGE IN HEAVEN

PART I

[- 1 -]

THE train clanked mile after mile through a lost country of marsh and vineyard among the foothills of the Pyrenees. Adrian Douglas sat at breakfast, twisting a brown hank of hair, staring with dark eyes at nothing.

There was someone he might claim to know on the train. Last night he had seen that girl Linet in a second class carriage, reading, so clean, so bright, so composed among strangers. He had paused on his journey from the dining-car to the sleeper, already lonely among the dense and ghostly hills, debating whether he should address her, a girl seen at parties, practically an acquaintance; but he was difficult with new people, especially girls, and this one, this honey-haired one, this swift and fairylike young person, could not possibly be within reach: and he didn't want her, or any girl, after all. She was not aware of his existence, he fancied; she never gave him a glance, was never likely to. He felt humble and without aspiration, as if she were a person such as one might imagine, but never hope or even wish to possess in this world.

In addition, it would be cowardly to seek her and talk to her because he was a little oppressed by solitude, he, a broad-shouldered, deep-breathing

9

man, surely able to dominate his feelings and thoughts. Anyone watching as he sat over his breakfast would have supposed him self-contained. The head was well shaped, well poised and unusually still. He had dark brown hair with a tinge of copper in it, a straight and decided nose, a firm, a rather obstinate chin. The lips were well made and sensitive; apt in moments of contemplation to purse a little sensually. The eyes, brown, green in strong light, under full lids, had a curious depth and unmoving intentness, as if he saw more in objects than their appearance. He was evidently a man of great stillness and concentration, subject to disruptive passions. He should have been engaged at this minute in a kind of strenuous sense-dreaming, less thought than an effort to divine the form and meaning of things: for him, the world one saw was a sign of something else. But sometimes that feeling of the relative existence of things turned to fear, fear of the unfamiliar, fear of the universe in which the mind found itself, fear, in moments when he was about to grasp difficult meanings, of meaning itself; and his mind fled for refuge to something recognizable, his own home, familiar people. And last night when he lay down alone in his sleeper and the train rattled in the heat of a summer night through steamy, suffocating hills, he asked himself, What am I, and what is it to have being? And he had fearful insights and breathed fast and sweated as people do when they think of time going on and on.

This morning, this brilliant hot morning, he

woke up nervy, and it was irritating that he could not enjoy the scenery with a peaceful mind. On his left the Mediterranean shone, blue and empty, brimming to harsh and desolate beaches. On his right marshes stretched, reedy remnants of the sea, and naked villages squatted by their shores in isolation. Beyond the marshes there were hills, and beyond the hills shapes of mountains, and there – he caught sight of it and his heart jumped – clouds opened on a gleam of snow and there seemed to be huge masses and height.

Suddenly he banged on the table. I will get over this, he said to the crumby plate. There's something wrong, or why should mountains make me emotional? I will get so that I have no fear left, and I shall be completely calm if I find myself in the middle of China or on the moon, or suddenly talking to trees. He rose and made his way back to the sleeper.

On his way through the second class compartment he couldn't help glancing in at the carriage where he had seen that girl last night. Yes, there she was, in a clean shirt, neat as a nit. She saw him, and slipped out into the corridor, cool and smelling of pine soap. 'Hullo!' she said.

'Hullo,' said he, snatched out of all misgiving by the sight of her.

'What are you doing?' she asked.

'I've just had breakfast.'

'No, I mean, where are you going?'

'Barcelona. I've got some work there. And

11

there's an Exhibition — tapestries and altar furniture and stuff. And you?'

'I'm going to stay with friends in Andorra. I get out at Gerona, I think.'

'Don't you know?'

Linet smiled back. 'There will be someone on the station.'

Adrian was astonished that she seemed so ready to come out and talk with him. Perhaps, he thought, she is bored with the long journey. But he desired to go on with the conversation, for she had a freshness and a fineness that pleased him. 'Have you had breakfast?' he asked.

'I'm too hard up.'

'Oh!' He touched her hand. 'Let me give you some.' He blushed crimson then.

'Are you rich or hard-up?' she enquired, watching him like a bantering insect.

'Hard-up. Extremely, sometimes.'

'Now?'

He reflected that although he had plenty of money with him there had been searching questions from the bank about his overdraft. 'Yes,' he said.

'Then you shall give me breakfast.'

Delighted, and confused, he led her to the restaurant. She sat opposite, chin on hand, watching while he ordered her breakfast. She wore a wedding-ring . . . he had heard she was married, and other talk . . . it scarcely seemed to be his affair. For once he found conversation easy. She ate slowly, and with great enjoyment; forgetting

12

her food, though, when she had a point to make. Adrian was happy. It was so light and yet so full of meaning, this conversation. They found agreement on all sorts of important small things.

He tried, without any appearance of staring, to study her looks. She could certainly be called pretty; more. Not beautiful, if you took feature by feature; but beauty, strict beauty, became a matter of no significance. What made her so attractive? She used no make-up: it would have been a pity to daub that excellent texture, or disguise the subtle tints of her mouth. He looked at her hair. It was honey-coloured, you might say, with glittering bright threads in it. And in a way it was green hair, as if she were a little bit immortal. It flowed beautifully from the crown — he had done angels' heads like that. Her eyes, too — they were brown, like his own, and green, greener than his; and sometimes gold. She had gold eyes in some lights, and they looked at him like the strange eyes of a fairy. Yes, there was certainly something rare in her substance; she had a peculiar fragrance and fine quality of flesh, as if she were fairy-bred, so to say. One would kiss a girl like that if she had just been picked up out of a drain.

Anyone watching them would have said they made an attractive pair.

After breakfast they strolled back. They might as well go on talking as far as Gerona, he thought. 'Come and see where I live,' he suggested.

He showed her his first class sleeper, now made

tidy for the day. She turned swiftly at the door, like a lizard. 'You said you were hard-up.' A frown came between her eyebrows.

'So I am.'

'You can't be, travelling in luxury like this.' There was a little scorn in her voice.

'I went a bust,' he explained. 'I wanted to see what it was like.' He couldn't explain that it was a device to protect himself from alien personalities with solitude, and from solitude with comfort. 'I made a bit of money, and decided to blow it,' he said. In any case, he was the son of a Highlander, intolerant of conditions and extravagant. At the same time he inherited something frugal: he understood at any rate the theory of thrift.

'I do that when I get money.' Linet smiled again and sat down in his compartment, stretching herself like a cat. 'I love this really,' she said. 'I was born to luxury. What are you?'

'I make windows. Stained glass.'

She showed interest. 'You're an artist. I wish I was.'

'I never think of myself as an artist,' he replied. 'I don't feel like one. . . .'

'You're clean and well dressed and efficient.' She looked him over. 'You look as if you like air and exercise.'

'I do a job of work, that's all.'

They talked, with window and door wide open because of the heat. She stretched out her legs in front of her. What a delicious, spindly creature!

And the line of her shoulders was excellent. And her bosom most sweet and shapely. They talked all the way, and changed trains together at the frontier.

'We're in Spain now,' said Linet.

Adrian looked out at the vines and olive trees scratched into red mountains, and down at the blue sea. They sat in a wide saloon in red plush armchairs. Adrian drank lager beer and Linet lemonade. The train wound its way out of the mountains, and soon they were looking back to the cloud-mantled ranges across rich plains where the corn had been harvested in June. The heat was intense, the sunlight dazzling. There were houses with pink walls, verandas with green blinds, and heavy tiled roofs. Oxen drew the plough, boys splashed naked in what summer had left of the rivers, and everyone was brown. Once, when Linet was gazing out of the window, he saw a look of deep sadness on her face. Yes, she was young and fine; and there was a shadow of cruel experience on her. But she didn't preoccupy herself with her thoughts. They talked until the train drew into Gerona, where some young people waved from the platform. Linet dashed to her carriage, tore down her luggage, and leapt out hatless. Adrian threw the hat after her. 'Good-bye,' he said.

'Good-bye,' she answered. 'It was nice to meet like that.'

'Very nice,' he agreed.

The train moved on. Adrian waved from the window, and noticed that the porters and people

15

on the platform were staring at the slim figure in the bright shirt. He returned to his seat, quite taken up with the vision of her. And it was extremely fortifying to his personality that he pleased her. It was some little time before he remembered his resolution, taken some three years before, that no woman should ever again distract him from the practice of his art. But in any case she was remote from his life and desire.

[- 2 -]

AT midday in mid-June in Barcelona, a torrid
white city among mountains, the heat was oppressive. Adrian put up at the Ritz, because it looked
friendly; but the luxury of that suite on the first
floor, that high and magnificent room with two
beds, that white and silver bathroom, that vestibule
with hatstand and settee, the convenience and
amplitude of the appointments and service, were
out of all proportion to what he could really afford.
The restaurant was shaded, open on one side to a
green alley with high wall of vine leaves and cle-
matis, and cold water sluiced the glass roof. After
luncheon a *valet-de-chambre* told him in a difficult
mixture of French and Spanish that it was inadvis-
able to be active during the afternoon; he lay naked
on his bed, therefore, in a green light that flowed
through the shutters, slightly tormented by flies.
Flies buzzed about the enormous space of the room
like aeroplanes in a shadowy green sky. There ought
not to be flies in this rich place. He suddenly
wondered at his own audacity. There must be a
powerful dose of folly or madness in me, he thought,
to hire this expensive suite. What would Linet say?
She would be up on the top floor, in the cheapest
room. She wouldn't be here at all, but in some
cheaper hotel.

What a pity money made such a difference.

B   17

Supposing, for example, she were staying in Barcelona, there was no reason, except her financial scruples, why she shouldn't have the other half of his suite. There it was for her, free. He was setting aside for the moment all other considerations, isolating this aspect of the financial scruple. But for that she might very well take her siesta on the other bed. And going a little farther on this path, one could easily imagine an ætherial green world like this where people could have fairylike and inconsequential relations. Adrian was floating off to sleep. A tap dripped in the bathroom. Relations without responsibility, without attachment, without suffering. The self would remain disengaged and inviolate. He slept.

About five o'clock he went out to the church that he was filling with windows, and called on the English resident through whom the work had come to him. This man, a traveller, a calm, Roman-Catholic man named Huxtable, had seen windows of Adrian's in New York. He praised what Adrian had done. It always embarrassed Adrian to hear his work discussed. He shrank from criticism, that seemed an act of impudence towards his personality; and distrusted praise, that always in some degree misunderstood his intentions. He knew that he had done nothing final. Huxtable said: 'You have a great future, I think. There is still something irrelevant in your work, formless and not genuine; but you have genius, I believe. I pity you.'

Adrian pitied himself. The responsibility of his

own powers dismayed him; for he felt them, imprisoned and mixed up as they were with what was vain in him.

'Praise will someday be given to your work when you have liberated it from yourself,' Huxtable said. 'In the meantime, what you do is very satisfactory. But I might wish to have lived a bit later.'

The man was detached and self-sufficient; or perhaps he relied on revealed truth. His eyes had borrowed a little of the steady judgment of Heaven. He took Adrian, who was trying to escape from the argument, to dinner in his house where he lived alone on the scented outskirts of Barcelona, among gardens and trees. At sundown the scent of flowers was overpowering; it rose over all the neighbourhood like a mist. Huxtable had lived many years in Mexico and his house was filled with curious objects; the rooms were crowded with strange furniture and dusky hangings, the lights were rich and dim, there was a smell of incense. A Mexican girl served dinner in the garden under spreading trees with deep-hued lanterns, and they sat long afterwards while the moon hung over the Mediterranean in a pansy-black sky. Adrian had a queer feeling that they must have been transferred to some other planet. He cured his vertigo with red wine and the vision of Linet, who gave him self-confidence.

'Do you work altogether on your own?' Huxtable asked.

'No, in association with others.'

'One would think there must be many working together to produce great stuff in glass.'

'There must; under a master, perhaps. I began under a master who wasn't a master. My uncle, as a matter of fact. He's dead now, and I rather take charge. Not so much because I want to, as that there's nobody else who will. As a matter of fact, I like the business end of it — sometimes, at any rate. One is two people, I suppose; several people.'

'More exactly?'

'I mean, sometimes I'm given over to seeing and creating; sometimes I spend weeks mucking about with new processes; and then, I must say I like running the shops, looking into costs and things.'

Huxtable listened and pondered. 'It's obvious you have a strong will,' he said. 'One that can't help but effect itself. I suppose an artist of real capacity must necessarily have a powerful and remorseless will, with the unexpected addition of a strong humility. There must be a surrender of the self to the self. . . .'

'I understand you,' Adrian broke in.

'I relate your experience, perhaps? And your inspiration — if you will excuse the word — does that come strongly, and unasked?'

'Oh yes! But I can bring it on, usually. I have a technique for that. . .' He suddenly perceived that he was undergoing examination, permitting a trespass, and disengaged himself from the theme.

20

Then all at once, when he had shut himself off from this stranger and their talk ceased, it seemed unbelievable that he was sitting under the dark trees, in this musky lantern-light, in a hot and florid planet. Why did things take this shape here, congealed for an instant out of nothing? He had no sensation of dread with these thoughts, for his personality had in some way been strengthened and reassured.

3

ADRIAN was not at all surprised to see Linet in the Ritz. She was bound to turn up somewhere sooner or later, like a fine day; he half expected to meet her in the torrid streets, among the flower stalls, composed and interested. She would be composed and interested if she were set down in the middle of China, or on the moon.

She was sitting all fresh and cool in the sluiced and shaded restaurant, attacking a hunk of iced cantaloup. She reminded him of lilies of the valley; but it was evident that she had appetite.

Adrian liked the look of her companions — a big, good-humoured, brown-faced man with dark, divining eyes; a well-bred, distinguished looking woman (his wife, one supposed); and four young persons of the kind that is used to the best of everything.

How nice for them to have her to stay, thought Adrian. And what a magnificent holiday it must be for her, to stay with these well-to-do people in a pink and orange house with green tiles and green sun-blinds among the foothills of the Pyrenees — that was how he pictured it. They would bathe in a winding river, under sweet chestnuts. Was Linet's husband there too? Or some other man? He suddenly felt a distinct and surprising pain. No, not any other man; nor a husband. One thought

22

of Linet as a fairylike person who, if she had passions, might have a passion for a tree; not for a man of this earth. Except perhaps momentarily by some accident of fancy. Adrian had an impulse to leave the restaurant, for that scene was idyllic and should be left untouched; he would prefer never to see her again, but to think of her for ever attacking a cantaloup and laughing with those pleasant people in the midst of a summer holiday.

She saw him and waved her spoon, with a beckoning gesture. Adrian was shy, but there was nothing for it: he must go to her table. She was out of her chair with a twist, and they were shaking hands. 'Is this where you're staying?' she asked.

'Yes.'

She seemed mocking; but it was difficult to read her eyes. To-day they were green eyes; or perhaps they reflected the green garden outside. There was a yellow point of sunshine in them. It was like being looked at by something among leaves.

He was introduced to the Mansfields and invited to sit down at their table. He accepted, and began with a slice of iced cantaloup as big as Linet's. It really was pleasant to have lunch with that dominating man, and those women in such elegant simple frocks. They were hospitable, open-hearted people; and the two youths and the two girls seemed well brought up. The parents had definite ideas, Adrian perceived, as well as fine manners. There were four or five younger children at home, he gathered. Those at the table were called Marigold, Viola,

23

Andrew and Bob. Eight or nine altogether! Mrs.
Mansfield had survived with distinction. She was
still a beauty, with delicate features and a delicate
colour, and a glance for her husband. And what
friendliness there was between all of them, a friendliness in which Linet belonged! What happy times
they must have in that pink house! It must be a
castle, with the governess and maids.

'We are staying here,' said Mrs. Mansfield. 'We
came over for the Exhibition. Have you seen it?'

'Yes. Marvellous, specially at night! Exhibitions
are meant for the night, don't you think? They
look a little unreal by day, but at night the world
changes and becomes unreal to suit them.'

'I quite agree,' Mrs. Mansfield replied, while her
husband, behind his good humour, seemed to read
Adrian's mind and character. Really, he had eyes
like a god's. 'This is the climate for Exhibitions,
I should think,' he observed.

'It is, certainly, with the heat and the deep
Mediterranean sky. But you must go by day, to
see the tapestries and images and silver candlesticks.' It was wonderful that Linet should be
staying here in the same hotel.

'Is there a switchback?' asked Bob.

'I do hope Mr. Douglas will come with us and
show us everything,' said his mother, 'if we are not
inflicting ourselves. To-morrow, perhaps?'

It was agreed, and life felt good. Adrian's nature
throve in the presence of people like these, affluent,
genuine and gifted; he enjoyed the climate. It

24

was pleasant that they seemed to like him. 'I hope you'll come and see my church?' It would be nice; particularly if the vanishing Linet accepted his invitation.

'Certainly we'll come,' said Mr. Mansfield. 'What do you do with a church?'

'I've done a Virgin, a Crucifixion, and three Saints so far,' said Adrian, 'with five medallions.'

The mouths of the four young ones opened a little, and Linet explained.

'I thought he was something to do with art,' said Marigold, the tall, fair girl (he was beginning to distinguish her from her darker sister), 'but I wasn't sure. It might be modern industry — something electrical.'

Adrian smiled. 'It is certainly an industry, making stained glass; but not modern. At least, I'm modern. I've invented some new things. You shall come and see it done some day, if you like.'

'I think you will probably have to have us all,' said Mr. Mansfield. 'Personally, now I'm in contact with the art, I want to know all about it.' And he would know all about it in a very short time, Adrian thought.

'So do I,' said Viola, a slim, dark-haired girl of (as Adrian guessed in spite of her composed manners) an ardent nature and intelligence. 'I knew he wasn't in anything electrical,' she added. 'I felt certain he was a painter or a writer.' She talked to Adrian quite eagerly during lunch, and he liked her. He admired the really distinguished flower-pattern of her frock. Andrew, the eldest son, a blunt-faced young man of positive character, signified that he was prepared to see the windows, and it was decided that they should drive out to the church late that afternoon, after the siesta. In the meantime, they parted. Adrian rode up in the lift with Linet and the Mansfield parents. 'Do you live on the first floor?' asked Linet, when he stopped the lift.

'Yes.' He felt at ease with her; even a little in command. 'I took a suite.'

'Oh!'

He grinned at her. The lift began to rise, and in a moment her feet disappeared beyond the ceiling.

He lay down in the heat and shuttered twilight of his grand room, and dreamt of her when he fell into a doze.

4

THE comparative darkness of the church was a relief from the glare outside. It was a rich darkness, because of the candle-points, the jewelled images and Adrian's windows. Adrian wondered what Mr. Mansfield was thinking of his great light-gathering wheel in the transept with St. Paul in the middle of it and three archangels below. The man was cultivated and urbane; he had seen many windows, and many other things. And what did Linet feel? She stood gazing, and the blaze of the window made her eyes blind. She seemed far away, as if she were living in that golden city set in azure fields. Huxtable, the donor, had come into the church and was standing among them.

'Marvellous! Beautiful!' said Marigold and Viola; their father said, 'Fine window.' Adrian considered his window and saw that it was magnificent; and that it was a failure. There was little they could tell him about the window that he hadn't seen for himself. It no longer interested him, indeed; but he remembered now what he had wanted to achieve. Or rather, he saw that he had tried to achieve several things, and there was confusion of form. Form! It began to preoccupy him. He had been entangled in subject and manner, subject that was not really his, manner that he still imitated from

27

the past — oh yes, he looked ruthlessly at the glow-ing jewellery, and with passionate regret, now that Linet was there to judge with those glory-blinded, unhuman eyes of hers. He tried to see in his windows something of what he had hoped to create, some greatness that had perhaps crept there unknown to him. People had praised it; even Huxtable. Linet, still gazing up, with legs apart and hands clasped behind her back, wore a smile.

'It reminds me of Chartres,' said Mr. Mansfield. 'It's in the great tradition, certainly.'

Quite true. Adrian had been hypnotized by the glory of those windows; he had vied with time in the production of blue and ruby and brown and lilac; but he could not obtain the same hue and melan-choly. Yet without doubt the geometrical pattern in the three windows beneath the rose-window deserved recognition. The great wheel itself turned in a blaze of splendour; turned restlessly, as if the saint in the middle were not quite in control. But the three archangels beneath, with brown intent faces, were sombre and still, like Boddhisatvas. And Huxtable had pointed out that St. Paul himself, in the centre of the wheel, dark faced and heavy-lidded, seemed as if he awoke from contemplation, like some Indian saint.

Linet, waking from her own queer dream, asked if he was satisfied with the window.

'No,' he answered. 'I can't say I am. I've just understood that I'm not really at home with these ecclesiastical subjects. I must try insurance offices.'

28

He sighed. It was God who had baffled him. He had no knowledge of God. Sometimes, in the quiet and dusk of a church, he wished to know God and reveal Him in some terrific window.

'How much easier it would be,' he said, 'if one could simply accept the traditional subject of some living religion; if one didn't have to look for one's subject in oneself.'

'Exactly,' said Huxtable. 'There will be no great art until men find their subject in Heaven. And to you I might say that there is no cause in sense or logic or any sort of science why you shouldn't find inspiration in the Roman faith.'

'I feel that sometimes,' said Adrian. 'But there's something that stops me — something quite definite. I feel there's something still more far-reaching and rooted in my constitution than that faith. I must unbury it.' The others were listening with attention — Andrew, he noticed, the blunt-minded Andrew, stared a little. He realized that he was giving himself away, and stopped. But his feelings rose within the sudden control of silence; and now he addressed words to himself — there are powers in me that must be allowed to work of themselves and I will not have the impertinence to stand in their way; this vision is laid on me as destiny, especially now that Linet had seen this failure; I won't rest until I have convinced Linet.

But sober thoughts returned soon: there were truths that he had thoroughly recognized. I shall never convince Linet, he said, with the work of my

29

hands, while that is my object; never create a fine window until the wish to do so has left me.

'I think he did see his window in Heaven,' said Linet, surprisingly.

He made a little gesture.

'Why are you in despair? I've never seen flowers like that in windows before.' So she had been directing her rapt eyes to the flower-borders, the leaf-borders, that he had so much loved making.

'His canopies and borders are at present the best part of his work,' said Huxtable. 'He'll do something remarkable if he finds himself and doesn't fall in love.'

'Only a fool would do that anyway,' Linet replied, and Adrian, who theoretically agreed with her, was surprised that her words gave him such a shock.

'Have you seen the Madonna yet?' Huxtable asked.

'Not yet.' They went to a chapel behind the high altar, a chapel green with hart's tongue and maidenhair, and saw Adrian's Madonna in the dimmer light, a Madonna seated among leaves in contemplation of water-lilies, a window like living ivy, of a deep greenness and secrecy. Adrian stared at the window himself, puzzled by what he saw there.

'One would say,' said Huxtable, 'that he might perhaps fall in love with a plant.'

'That would be more sensible,' Linet remarked. 'He has a queer mind, I must say. His Madonna isn't at all what you look for; not in the least like a Madonna.'

'No,' said Huxtable, pointing out what had puzzled Adrian, 'the remarkable thing is that she's like you.'

5

AFTER a long day they dined in an orange grove. Later, when the party split up, Linet and Adrian found themselves walking among glowing pylons towards a palace illuminated on a mountain. They climbed by grove and terrace, under cascades of fire and cypresses of water, to the resplendent summit. For a little while they strolled in the Spanish Town. They were in Granada, in Orvieto, Valladolid, Guadalajara. They climbed a steep, night-bound street in Seville, and faces of Spanish women peeped at them from the darkness behind southern ferns. At the top there would be a glimpse of the slow Guadalquivir — no, it was night in Toledo, in Saragossa; romantic escutcheons emblazoned noble doorways; there was the tower of a church faced with shimmering tiles; they went in by the black entrance of a monastery and walked in musty cloisters; they stood by a well from some far and melancholy province; a star-struck Madonna smiled on a wall. Then, growing weary, they retired into the darkness and quiet of a hanging garden that looked over the city, and sat down under the walls of some castle in Spain. The night was musky. Before them palaces were outlined in light, white towers burned in a black sky, illuminated cascades streamed forth from nothing, jets of bright rain swayed and changed on the air, there was a faint flow and clashing of water, and a tree of fire, leaf-green, lemon-yellow, poppy-red, grew up to heaven. Behind in the Spanish Town they heard a thrum of guitars and a high voice chanting; and if for a few minutes silence fell nightingales sang in the groves.

'I feel as if I were back at school and having a treat,' Linet said. It was like a cat's voice talking under the trees.

'You're still much of a child in some ways,' Adrian replied, 'and in some ways very much grown-up, I should think.' It was strange to have the company of this slim and elegant young woman. 'I feel very young myself,' he said.

'You look it,' she answered. 'Sometimes you have a very young look.' In a world of marvels they both felt like children; took hands and stared at the fountains glowing and fading, the cascades and trees of fire. Adrian was surprised to notice that, with Linet beside him, in a world of illusion he felt more than ever himself.

Rockets sprang from a distant mountain, and climbed a black sky in which there could be seen no other stars; the universe outside and beyond this world of orange trees and violet cascades was empty. Linet found an example or text in the fireworks. 'The shape of life changes,' she said. 'Everything gives way to something else. One must accept that. One must never try to keep anything.'

Adrian knew thoughts of this kind; but he felt

c   33

sharp disappointment that Linet should be so obedient to change. 'It's easy to make these comparisons,' he replied; 'but I don't quite understand in what sense things really pass, or where they go. But I'm no philosopher.'

'Love especially is like that,' Linet went on. 'I don't mean that love is foolish; it isn't; it's beautiful, and I've been in love. But people are foolish if they wish to keep it, or to possess each other; foolish and ignoble.'

Adrian felt intensely sad and desperate at her words. It was true that the substance departed from things, leaving only a garment of illusion. He remembered experiences of the afternoon, dim and memorylike now day was gone. They had walked through gallery after gallery crowded with objects from centuries of Spanish history — tapestries, armour, vestments,.sacred effigies, shrines and rich ecclesiastical furniture. Adrian had found it a ghostly and oppressive place, a musty remnant of what had been glittering and handsome when the blood was in it, the jewelled cerecloth of what was well-fleshed and magnificent when it lived. And those twelve tableaux, those waxen memorials — one had seemed to look back through some tremulous medium of time at the spectres of legendary men. Had priests that authority once, kings that dominion, captains that wrath? This scene was unforgettable — majesty seated in a tent, the minatory cardinal in scarlet, the crowd of dark faces brooding beneath their visors, the lifted curtain,

the flash of breastplates and spearheads in a noon-
day blaze. And there were mysterious, religious
scenes and brilliant episodes with all the gold and
flush and vigour of fabulous courts. It seemed as if
all these figures had moved living into the past and
still enacted their gorgeous destiny, for ever contented with magnificence. Were they still somewhere there, and had they by jugglery been brought
back to the present, somewhat ghastly in their
resurrection?

It was unforgettable and it was obscene. Adrian
pushed it all from his memory, and turned his eyes
to the modern spectacle.

'Yes,' he agreed. 'Life passes and the body becomes hideous. Everything changes, and it is
foolish to preserve the garments of what is dead.
But one could wish it were not so.'

'Why?' He was aware that she looked at him for
a few moments, and he wondered what her thoughts
were. 'Many beauties are better than one surely?
And about love fading — it's a fact we have to face,
and if a thing is a fact there's nothing wrong about
it surely? One must just start from that in thought
and action.'

'Oh well! I myself believe that love needn't pass.'
He said it roughly and suggested that they should
walk. She agreed. Having descended the mountain, they resorted to a café and told one another
much, but not everything, about their lives and
opinions. Around them colonnades of glass glowed
purple, violet and yellow; fountains spurted and

clashed, and pearly grottoes glowed pinkly in the heart of a lake. Cascades poured from the mountain, terrace by terrace, and nightingales sang in the groves.

ADRIAN drove Linet home in a taxi, and they entered the luxurious hotel together. It seemed a pity to say good night when they were so friendly; they had a little more conversation, therefore, under the palm trees in the deserted lounge. 'I like sitting up all night,' said Linet, 'especially in the heat. I can't sleep.'

'My work suffers if I sit up all night.'

'Oh? Are you a slave to your work?' Her lips curled faintly.

'Yes,' he said. 'I am. I propose to be.'

'Well then — you'd better go to bed.'

'It happens I don't want to to-night.' He knew that when she went up in the lift it would end the day, and they might never meet again. But she insisted, whatever he said. It was almost a little quarrel.

'Then at least let's walk up by the stairs,' he said.

They mounted slowly. Linet had a habit if any thought engaged her of stopping where she was and thrashing the thing out. Perhaps she was deciding to change her mind and let him sit up. They came to the first floor. 'Would you like to see my rich suite?' he enquired.

'Oh yes.' They went along the passage. He unlocked the door, and turned on the lights in the ante-room, bathroom and bedroom. Linet's eyes

37

popped out on sticks. 'My word! What luxury!'
She examined the appointments, looked at the
sheets and pillowslips, played with all the taps in
the bathroom, and flung herself down like a child
in the big easy-chair. 'I'm tired!' she exclaimed.
Then she leapt up again. 'Sorry! I forgot you want
to go to bed.'

He smiled. 'Do you despise me for it?'

'Not a bit.' She held out a hand. 'Good night.
But oh! May I just go out on the balcony?'

Adrian pulled back the shutters and they stood
together on the balcony for a minute, watching the
flats opposite. 'I really must go,' she said at last.
'Good night. I may not see you before we go.'

'Good night, then, and perhaps good-bye.' He
was airy too. It was necessary. He saw her to the
lift. As he returned to his room a night-porter
grinned. Adrian stopped. 'Swine!' he said to the
non-comprehending functionary. 'Swine!' He
slammed his door, and raged. But he remembered
the talk there had been about her.

Now evil had shewn its face, casting foul eyes on
what was sweeter than anything Adrian had hoped
to see; and now he must listen to the daemon that
answered in his own heart.

ADRIAN waited for his visitors at the front-door, under the portico between pillars, surveying the quiet road beyond the gravel drive and the stripped limes. It was towards midday on a fine Friday morning, moist and warm, in November; the shrubberies glistened as if they had been washed; their winter green reigned in full health and vigour now that summer leaves had vanished into the mud. Adrian was house-proud. He stepped into the drive and surveyed the mansion, an ample if exuberant mansion, with square tower and wings and greenhouses, islanded among shrubberies in a triangle of leafy roads, just where the wealthy regions of St. John's Wood border on a more dismal neighbourhood. The mansion was many-windowed, well-painted and well seen to, classical, with fluted columns, heavy entablature, and wall spaces made interesting with some architectural device; in particular there was something solid and Roman in the smaller two-storied wing that turned back from the main part of the house. Ivy clung there; and the first design had been a little confused with the addition of a circular glass-house. Confusion, indeed, or a rather pleasing wealth and variety of idea, was the chief character of the house; and there was confusion in the garden, where holly trees grew with limes, and tall privet encircled a melancholy lawn.

It was here that Adrian and Mark Scoby his cousin conducted their business. Mark's sister Bella kept house. Every morning the craftsmen came in by a side door among the shrubberies, and rooms and passages and cellars in the rearward parts of the mansion were filled with people cutting, leading, soldering, painting, and baking confections of glass. The other rooms, the reception rooms, the main bedrooms and dressing-rooms were kept for the most part as they had been in the days when Mark's father had lived there with Mark's mother. Bella had her bedroom and small sitting-room; Mark his. Adrian had rooms in the tower, with private access through a small door in the drive.

Mark was a man of fantastic ugliness who fulfilled himself in a hobby: he knew all about the civilizations of the Middle East. He had a low broad forehead with a fringe of hair, a huge and slobbery mouth with a fringe of teeth the top row of which inclined outwards as if meant for shoving away snow. His nose was gnarled and his ears were enormous; his face often looked like an old root. But pale eyes glimmered in the midst of it in a manner so innocent and affectionate that people loved him. In glass, he had no originality: his work was done under direction.

Bella, Mark's sister, was not ugly, but no man had ever thought of her as a bride. She had suffered much pain during the last twenty years, and had twice submitted to a major operation; yet she never let herself off any work. Her face was much changed through pain, and not for the worse. Adrian often wondered how she managed to be so cheerful and kind; but she was a stranger, kept at a distance from his mind and senses, for pain horrified him. It was not necessary, he knew, to suffer in the mind; mind-suffering was a mere after-headache of desire. But anguish of the body — that was a sign of cruelty in the nature of things; an earnest of more terrible possibilities, lying in wait perhaps for the dead.

Many thoughts arose in Adrian's mind while he waited for the visitors. It had become clear to him that his work demanded that he should know himself and hide no facts whether they existed within him or without. It would soon be necessary, he saw, to face this problem of pain. But during these last weeks he had been examining his mind in regard to Linet. He could not be in love, for he felt no jealousy; he was benevolent towards her; he would be glad to know that she was enjoying herself, in whatever way. He remembered, too, that he was no longer free to fall in love, and all those desires of the flesh and longings of the spirit that had once tortured him were employed in other service. Perhaps, he admitted in a moment of extreme candour, I dare not be jealous, because the jealousy that might arise in this case would destroy me. Indeed, he was aware of some strong passion expressing itself in unusual creative activity. But the new ideas that he got through that severed contact with her were still confused; and in the moments of absolute honesty that the artist above all men knows he was aware of destined failure before he had well begun. Not for the form's sake was he working, but for her sake; not for what beauty might arrive, but in self-regard, adding impertinent splendours to his theme. Thus he saw that it was right to cut himself off from Linet altogether, and deflect the powers that she had aroused in him to the service of art.

But a fortnight ago he had run into Mr. Mansfield on the steps by the Duke of York's column, and suddenly asked his address. Then he wrote and invited the Mansfields to inspect the factory and celebrate their meeting at Barcelona with luncheon: and it was only polite to ask Linet as well. And now here they were in the drive, and Linet was with them, in green, like a cutting from the shrubs.

Greetings were enthusiastic. Only two of the young people had come — Marigold and Viola. Andrew was at work and Bob back at school. In any case six would be too many to force on them for lunch, Mrs. Mansfield said. The two girls looked very pretty and well turned out in their London clothes, and as for Linet, it seemed as if some shrub-fairy had got into the house. It was pleasant to be in such favour with these three. Adrian introduced Bella and Mark, and forthwith conducted the party through the workshops. Mark hovered in the background, sabre-toothed and enthusiastic, like something that does not quite belong to the human race. Mr. Mansfield asked questions about the processes and the management of the business. His eyes penetrated everywhere, among things and persons; he seemed to possess an enormous openness and decision, and to expect these qualities in others. Adrian answered him and tried not to pay too much attention to Linet, who glided·from room to room, and displayed affection for the cat, and listened in the manner of a respectful wraith; and it was only when she was compelled to ask for a clean rag that he found she had cut her finger in the glazing-room, quietly using an odd cutting tool on an odd piece of glass.

'Most interesting!' Mr. Mansfield said. 'Is your rent heavy?'

'We don't pay any,' Adrian told him. 'Except ground rent. The house is ours.'

'The lease would be difficult to dispose of, I should think.'

Adrian admitted that it was so, and led the party upstairs. In a darkened theatre, high up under the roof of the mansion, by means of an alterable window and with the help of two men in aprons, Adrian displayed windows or portions of windows — saints, angels with trumpets, martyrs, ascetics, demons, sages, glimpses of heaven and studies in terrestrial landscape. There were patterns of flowers and leaves, too, and patterns in clear glass and lead. 'There isn't much demand for all this kind of thing that one might like so much to do,'

43

he said. 'It's mostly sacred windows, with portraits of the donor. I wish I could get more work for libraries and public buildings. There's a great future for glass in public buildings, secular buildings I mean, if people would realize it.'

'What lovely things!' Viola said, and he saw her dark eyes gazing. But Adrian was suddenly depressed over his work, although the visitors praised it. True, that even in the work that had to be done in compromise with the wishes of those who paid for it his power could not be hidden, and his personality was visible in the whole output of the factory; true that his colours were rich and sombre and suffused with strange light; that there was mystery in his glass, a more than human magnificence and resignation, with a certain terrible intentness, in the faces of his saints; true that his flower designs and his patterns of clear glass and lead were delightful; he was discontented, nevertheless, and moved with some undiscovered trouble. It was a relief to have to forget it, and entertain the visitors.

They gathered in Adrian's own work-room in the tower for sherry before lunch. It had windows on three sides, and views over roofs and tree-tops to the hills beyond London.

'Do you sleep in this tower?' Linet asked.

'My bedroom is immediately below. There's a bathroom too — I had it put in.'

'You're a luxurious fellow,' said Mr. Mansfield. 'How do wages run in your industry?'

44

'Pretty high,' Adrian said, hiding with calm face the secret knowledge that the upkeep of this mansion swallowed too much of his profits. He began to think that this Mr. Mansfield was a little greedy for knowledge.

'It's a delightful and most interesting establishment,' Mrs. Mansfield said. 'But what a labyrinth of a house!'

'I find it a little strange and gloomy,' said Linet, 'with all those men working like gnomes in caves, and the holly trees on the terrace. Of course, it's rather a moist, gloomy sort of evergreen day.'

'I like moist, evergreen days,' said Adrian, as they went down through corridors crowded with old furniture and busts on pedestals to the dining-room. 'Don't you?'

'No, I like sunshine and heat.' It was difficult to remember that he and she had been so friendly among the fireworks. The mountains, the corn, the dried rivers, the heat and blaze of Barcelona had now the remoteness and illusion of those tableaux. This luncheon party, too, would soon have moved into the past; they would be nothing but figures sitting at table, in an unearthly light. The dining-room, indeed, was already a relic, furnished in the days of Bella's parents with grand mahogany table and sideboard, rich leather-covered chairs, fine carpet and noble clock. The leather was worn thin and the carpet faded, but the mahogany glowed and the clock ticked and chimed in full vitality. Two long windows gave on the drive, shrubs reached to the little verandas, a kind of small and spreading lime tree grew in a pot between the curtains, and there were green claret-glasses on the table.

An acting parlour-maid served the dishes. Adrian felt pleased with his establishment and wondered whether the business could be made to afford a substantive parlour-maid. It was odd that an artist should be so fond of solidity and regular form.

'How do you manage to keep brown and weatherbeaten?' asked Linet. 'You were brown in Spain, naturally; but people usually lose their brown by November.'

'Adrian's complexion is always brown. He is fond of fresh air and exercise.' It was Bella who spoke, as if she were his mother.

'A little Indian,' said Linet, but she may have been thinking of his intent and contemplative expression. Indeed, his thoughts were away. The life dies out of everything, she had said, leaving a musty remnant. Adrian protested, he who in youth had thought that love would be for ever. It was queer that side by side with those longings there should have existed such passions. There were dark places in the geography of his being, Adrian knew; but closed at present.

While these thoughts passed he was in conversation with Mrs. Mansfield, and with Viola who with a sudden relapse from young womanhood asked if she could have a second helping of Russian jelly. Linet was enjoying her lunch too. Methodically and remorselessly she had disposed of alligator pears, scallops, chicken and sweets. Her food seemed much too big for her; she looked so fairy-like.

After lunch they all went to the drawing-room. Adrian wondered what Linet thought of the drawing-room. It had been necessary that they should give parties sometimes, on business; and for this purpose Adrian considered the drawing-room as occupied by Bella's parents unsuitable. He cleared out its whole contents therefore, and with the help of professional friends planned and executed a remarkable decoration.

The drawing-room extended along the whole of the west side of the house. Its three long windows gave access to a terrace; the terrace, flanked by holly trees, led down to the melancholy lawn. It was an elegant room, with polished floor and a minimum of furniture. The walls disclosed a continuous and unreal scene in which use was made of doors, pillars, mirrors and chimneypiece to divide, frame or emphasize. In the centre of the principal wall-space a sage meditated under a tree whose branches extended over the ceiling. On one hand cataracts fell harmoniously from pine-clad crags and snows gleamed beyond. On the other, swans floated among huge-bladed water-plants, and reedy marshes stretched towards a horizon. Between the windows cypresses grew among ruins, and temples crowned the summits of hills.

47

'I congratulate you,' said Mr. Mansfield. 'A remarkable room. It needs a bold mind to treat a drawing-room like that.'

'How beautiful!' Viola exclaimed. Adrian felt her wondering eyes on him. But his interest was all in what Linet would say.

'We paid for it with martyrdoms, crucifixions and last judgments,' he explained.

'It's a decoration of escape, of course,' Linet observed.

'No, it's an escape into reality,' Adrian replied. 'Quite different from crimson-ramblers.'

'You have a queer mind.' Linet looked long into the landscape. 'Carl would like it.'

'Carl?'

'My husband.'

'Well, I can invite him. Where does he live?'

'I haven't the slightest idea.'

'Oh!' Adrian paused. 'Would you give me your own address?'

'There's no point in your having it,' Linet said; and Mrs. Mansfield came over to insist that they must be going.

8

ADRIAN had not yet formally recognized a state of
being in love. He lived for these few weeks instinc-
tively, absorbed by events without reflecting on
them. Linet had refused her address; but she
provided him with a series of gratifying surprises.
First, she began coming to parties. He did not
assume that she did so in order to see him; for
although he had a confidence in his destiny that
might have been the confidence of some other being
within him, and although he was still subject in
many ways to the conceit of self-reference, he was
humble before his work and before Linet. But she
showed a disposition, at parties, to associate with
him, frankly, as if she had considered and made up
her mind about it. It was wonderful that the
vanishing Linet approached him, in all friendship,
and became the more mysterious the more he knew
her. She seemed unearthly; her life was all in
the mind and imagination.

It turned out that she lived close by in two rooms
of a house that overlooked Lord's Cricket Ground.
It was a long time before he saw them, for although
he walked or drove home with her several times
she didn't seem to want him to come in, and shook
hands at the door. He did not press her. Their
commerce was mental, an investigation of each
other's personality; and when they knew certain

D
49

things they might proceed to learn some other
things. During this time, there seemed to be no
bodily awareness and no jealousy. Once, it is true,
when they were shoved close together in the tube,
he had a sense of the sweetness and wonder of
her body; but he did not envisage it, or hope for it.
Curious, that the contact did not excite passion in
him, so much composed of earth.

One wet January afternoon she came to tea with
him in the tower. He boiled a kettle and made tea
with care, using the best he could find in London.
She looked so fair and young, gracefully disposed
in the window-seat under the rainy glass, with her
honey-coloured hair and her pale-blue shirt and
pleated skirt, that she became part of his vision for
ever, like something seen in a grouping of trees or
in some conjunction of afternoon clouds.·

'I'm glad you have flowers in your room,' she
said.

He sat near her and looked out of the window.
The sky was full of drizzle floating or falling; there
was ·a view over wintry roofs and tree-tops to a
horizon of rain.

'This view often reminds me of Northern France
on bleak days,' he said. 'Bailleul, for instance.
There are roofs, and I have an illusion of trees and
soggy fields beyond. I expect the flash of field-
guns.'

'Did you like that when you saw it?'

'Like it? Yes, I think I did.'

'Did you like the war?'

'Bits of it. I found myself, you see; at the very bottom of misery. It's reassuring to survive extremes. I was never happy before the war. I was a preposterous, impossible youth. Everyone said so, especially women. I had no sort of success in any department of being or activity, and I was terrified of the world and people. The war released me. Somehow it failed to split up my identity, and I've felt different since. Afraid, sometimes, still. But I'm talking too much.'

'Have you any people?'

'Not one, except Bella and Mark. My parents were ferocious, oppressive and inflexible, but they died during the war. My father was a parson; a Highlander. My mother came from East Anglia and was very practical.'

'I should think you could be ferocious, oppressive and inflexible yourself.'

'Do you?' He wondered. 'Tell me about your people.'

'In a minute. First, tell me how you became an artist.'

'How does one know that? I can only say that this window-making business existed on my father's side of the family and I could draw. I was allowed to come to London, under the care of my well-conducted uncle, and I attended art-schools and drew profusely and practised in the work-rooms here. My uncle was very moral, and his windows were awful. We still suffer from his influence. Now about your people.'

51

Linet laughed. 'We lived in Sussex, and my sisters and I never did anything but climb trees and ride and fish and wander about the country. We were happy, and I wish it was like that now. I grew up without noticing it, and for some reason I became engaged. He was in the Guards — rich, tall and extremely handsome with a beautiful fair moustache. I couldn't bear him really, so I hooked it, a week before the wedding. My people were mad and have stayed mad. I tried being a shop-girl. But I simply cannot stand doing the same thing day after day and having to keep hours; I'd rather starve. So I gave that up and since then I've done all sorts of things and just scraped enough money together to get myself a room and food and live my own life. Once I got married, to an Austrian. I don't know where he is now — back in Austria perhaps. Perhaps I'll tell you more about that another day, and perhaps not.'

There was a stopping short in Adrian's mind: it was necessary to become self-conscious for a moment and remind himself that the state of her heart towards that husband did not concern him.

They talked on and on, and met to talk again, seeking important information. It was always surprising and delightful that, yes, she was free the next afternoon, and could dine with him, fortunately, on Wednesday. It will end soon, he thought; it is too strange to go on. She will suddenly lose this interest, which can be no more than curiosity. He never realized that already they had gone far together; it came to pass without his remarking it that they were always deep in conversation, and had no engagements except with one another. He could not know what Linet felt. She gave him nothing whatever with her eyes, and her voice mocked if their talk became too serious. And now, when she mocked in this way, he began to experience a new agitation and despair.

She was surprised, perhaps, to discover her own state of mind; at any rate, the discovery sent her into exile.

One fine evening in April they went to the theatre and were happy. Linet was alight that evening. 'We're always happy together,' she remarked, like a child, and put her hand up to straighten his tie. During the second act an event like the sudden opening of a flower took place in Adrian's soul; he saluted the fact that without her society and conversation it would be impossible to live. It seemed urgent that he should tell her so, and as soon as they were in the taxi he put an arm round her shoulders. She leaned her cheek on his most naturally. Surely the press of her sensations was great and amazing like his own; but she accepted his kiss rather as if her thoughts were at a distance.

'I love you,' he said.

'One should not use that word,' she replied. 'I don't myself.'

It was chilling. But he desired her now at all costs. 'Let's pretend, then, for to-night,' he murmured.

53

'For to-night? For half an hour, if you like.' It was impossible to understand her. She was mysterious, alight and aloof; serious and mocking. He only felt that he was in favour with her will. Suddenly she took and kissed his face seven times, on forehead, eyelids, cheeks, mouth and chin. 'Does that satisfy you?' she asked. 'Here we are at my door. See you to-morrow perhaps?' She had shaken his hand now, and was gone. He paid the driver, and walked for miles through the April-scented roads, remembering her kisses.

9

APRIL breathed at the window. Adrian rose from
bed, bathed in great pleasure of the morning, and
wandered over the house, opening doors and windows to let in air and scents. Linet's mouth had
changed him; he felt tempered and delicate, as if
his cellular composition had been altered by some
radiation from the touch of her lips. His limbs were
springy and received influences from the earth
when he stood on the lawn; he listened with
solemn delight to a peaceable blackbird singing
among the new leaves. Was it too early to ring up
that dapper young woman? He thought of her
with delight — how she was fast as a fish in her
movements, elusive as the gleam of a fish in
water. She would come to the telephone from her
bed, sweet as April. And she would ask him to join
her there; she, so frank. Most frank Linet would be,
when her spirit was convinced. His thoughts
changed — he could not descry the future. It was
only certain that his mind was all towards Linet
and hers to him; each had eagerness for the other.
But her mind might have changed in the night.
This agitated him, and he walked on the terrace,
and in the drive, and then in the triangle of roads,
going farther from the telephone the more it drew
him.

Linet might even at this minute be on her way to

55

Victoria; he had a presentiment that she would vanish to France, or Italy, or Spain. Anxiety became too great and he telephoned. Would her voice answer? No, it was another voice. Was she in? The voice would see. He suffered, waiting for the returning feet. He could hear them now, shuffling towards his glued ear — not Linet's feet, then. Well? She would be down in a minute. At last Linet's voice, rather distant, rather patrician. Was she free for the day? Yes, for part of it. Yes, she would come to lunch.

All the morning Adrian found himself unable to work, and was ashamed of it. But again, to-morrow would be Good Friday, and art did not matter in the least in this world that was all Easter and Linet. There were flowers everywhere in the house, snowdrops, crocuses, and thickets of daffodils growing in bowls. Linet was delighted with them; she talked of nothing else. Flowers pleased her better than people, she said; they displayed no passion or possessiveness.

They had lunch by themselves at one end of the great mahogany table. Bella was ill in bed, and Mark had gone away for Easter. Linet was very polite and ceremonious, like a child on its best behaviour; and it was delightful to entertain her. They acted as if they had forgotten last night; yet from time to time there was evidence of pre-occupation behind their talk. After lunch they could not settle in any place, perhaps in fear that if they brought love to words it would escape. They wandered from room to room, and Linet plagued the men at their work with questions. In the firing-room, where the kiln was growing cold because of the Easter holiday, she mentioned that she was leaving next day for Bordighera.

'For Bordighera!'

'Yes. I might stay abroad. I might take a job in Paris.'

'You mean, you might never come back?'

'Yes.' She ran her fingers up the stem of a narcissus and pinched the flower.

She could not have understood. He took her arm. 'Will you come in here?' She glanced, and followed. He took her to the glass-house on its platform of stone that filled the angle between two wings of the mansion. A young draughtsman in an overall was watering the plants.

'What do you grow in here?' she asked.

'I grow orchids and poisonous plants, some dangerous, some mortal; hemlock, henbane, caper spurge, and deadly nightshade. You shall see them all one day when they're at their best, I hope. At present it's mostly orchids.' There were water-plants, too, in glass tanks.

The young man in the overall went away.

'What a lovely place! You have a strange mind!' She stared at him, speculating. Then she began with delight to inhale the moist smell, and to put her fingertips to the glistening substance of the orchids. How handsomely she stood, like a fencer, well planted on her legs, gripping the stone floor with

57

her feet. Shoulders and bosom were of a most graceful shape. He considered her nose, small and a little curved: one saw she was proud, and obstinate. He watched the small movements of her rose-tinted lips, that were so cool; and her eyes as she gazed into the translucent flowers. Her life was all in her gaze; the gold irises and black pupils dilated and contracted minutely with the fluctuations of her excitement. Now that he had her alone with him in this strange green place out of the world and common experience, he felt conviction. They must recognize one another here, strange creatures themselves, and recognition must be for ever.

There was silence. Outside, through the tinted glass, a sun blazed among shapes of trees. Within the glass-house life teemed in the vegetables and achieved itself in glorious existences; water dripped into a tank; and in the moist intoxicativeness and aphrodisiac smell of that glass chamber they had vision of something unattainable, beyond the marvel of flowers. He held her for a minute, not knowing whether she were plant or girl; she answered his kiss, and they seemed to understand all experience of all living things. They stood then apart in silence, and when he looked at her there were tears on her cheeks, big glistening tears with the green world in them.

'It hurts,' she said. 'It ought not to.'

At first Adrian did not know what to say: he had said everything. He had an instinct to relate their experience to the ordinary world. He opened a window, therefore, and they put out their two heads. Green vegetable stains ran down the stone wall that supported the glass-house, and disappeared among shrubs.

'There can't ever be anything else for me,' he told her.

'Everything changes.' She smiled, and took his hand tight like a child.

'I must go,' she said next.

'Oh no! Why must you go?'

Her eyes gave reassurance, and it was the more strange that she should insist on going, as insist she did.

ADRIAN woke in the fire of daybreak. Crocus-
purple clouds stood in the yellow fields eastward
across the trees; strange thoughts, mildewy, baneful,
poisonous, grew in the edges of his mind. He went
out to the garden, to breathe in the golden air;
he walked through leafy roads, in the silence and
heavenly solitude of early morning; he took April
and fiery trees and glimpse of blue distances into
himself with deep breaths; but the question would
not be consumed — Why did she go away? What
sort of a person is she? How can she be so light?

He knew, with the bright part of his nature,
that these doubts were unworthy; and it surprised
him that he had such strong evil in himself. She is
not light, he said; her very obstinacy is a sign. He
if anyone was light in human relationships, light
and deadly serious at the same time. An artist, his
realizations were vivid, and evanescent; he touched
something final in the universe, and it was gone;
what was convincing at the moment of insight
seemed incredible afterwards. His personality was
an arena in which there took place changes. For
him, all views dissolved. Not so with Linet, in spite
of her doctrines. From her lips he drank something
immortal. But then — she had kissed men before.
But surely, surely, it was with Adrian only that it
hurt! He quickened his step on the shining pave-

ment with thoughts and feelings all in confusion. I will go to Bordighera, that will be golden with mimosa. In a second, with some profound wisdom of which he was not yet conscious, not yet the possessor, he decided it was not the time for him to go after her. She had some reason for delaying their love; some elder friendship to dispose of. He asked whom else he should find in Bordighera, and went hot for shame of himself. Now indeed he saw that he must allay for ever that uprising savage.

In the afternoon he had to see a sad-eyed clergyman who had spoken to him in the road one morning about some windows. When he came back there might be a letter. It was urgent that the clergyman should give him an order, for things were in a poor way; but he went to the interview without much mind for it. The interview stimulated his ambition, nevertheless. The Reverend Eugene Pollock had built a library, for which he desired windows. 'I like your work,' he said, 'and I think you are coming to something better. You have richness, you understand melancholy, you possess insight. Give me sombre windows, and let them illustrate the great religious systems of the world. If there are not enough, invent some.' His pale eyes looked at Adrian over his glasses, and it was impossible to say whether he winked; one only felt there was some huge and tristful joke. 'Let there be brown, purple and ruby, and let there be ornament. Ponder these windows; submit yourself to the things that are within you, and bring me designs.'

Adrian went home in some excitement. The clergyman's faith in him was very supporting; and he began to think that a celibate devotion to art might have consolations for any human grief. Nevertheless, he looked in the hall for a letter.

There was no letter. Days passed, and he was out on the drive for every post. He began to be angry: she might at least send him a card. He had written himself the very day after her departure, a direct expression of his passion, a letter full of April, written on fine paper, with little paintings of flowers and angels' heads like her own. It was desolating that there should be no answer to this, and in a few days her silence reduced him to a point where it became a definite necessity to achieve self-conquest, or at least to lose himself in the contemplation of some great thing. I have failed to find peace, he said, in the contemplation of that minute with her in the glass-house; I would have wished to be a man who could do that, but I am not. I shall go to Chartres. His senses longed for the magnificence of that Church, for the height and spaciousness, the twilight silence, the gloomy splendour of the windows, and brightness of that great rose in the west. He could remember Linet there in tranquillity, taken out of himself into that greater Presence; their personal moment would take its place in the sad history of man, so majestic in its sadness; and perhaps he would be swept on some tide of music to shores where things are not lost. By this means he climbed up to the thought of something more stable than his own passions, and managed to exist in a region of wide survey and rarefied atmosphere, where the fear of losing his new, sweet friend was not intolerable.

But imagination would have to suffice, for, if he went to Chartres, Bella, who was ill, would be left alone. Mark was still away, at a congress of some kind where they discussed matters in which he was interested. The thought of Bella's sufferings helped to deprive Adrian of his own. She had pain without alleviation; and he had nothing after all — he was sure of it at moments — but a great joy that should no longer be confined and poisoned in the cavernous darkness of his nature. He went to her room. Bella was sitting in a chair at the table, with some needlework.

'You don't often come to see me,' she said.

'I know. Is there anything I can do for you now?'

'No, thank you, Adrian.'

Indeed, the room was quite strange to him, this small old-fashioned room with lace curtains that held the sunshine. There were flowers in it, and a bullfinch in a cage over the sewing-machine in the window. There was a miscellaneous collection of furniture, as if Bella had not cared about her surroundings; objects that perhaps the old people had discarded, objects from a generation before her own. Outside was the lawn, the holly trees: this glimpse pleased Adrian.

63

'How is your pretty friend?' Bella asked. 'You got on well, you two.'

'She has gone abroad. I don't know if she will come back.'

'She will,' said Bella.

It was beautiful to be named in the same breath with Linet. Was Bella foresighted? He waited with pleasure for what she would add, and realized that she was silent because for the moment she could not speak. He did not know what to do.

'What was I going to say?' asked Bella at last. She did not remember, or decided not to say it: but Adrian was kindled. 'She will,' Bella had said, undoubtedly with foreknowledge. Bella knew what he had not faith to know. Bella had married them. He was ashamed that the strong life in him could so easily forget her sickness.

He stayed with Bella all afternoon, and brought her supper; then worked half the night that he might not slip back into doubt. The night was so deep and magical that it seemed as if Linet must float in at the window. He spoke to her, and waited to hear some answer in the stillness. Three or four days Bella was ill, and it seemed wonderful to him that the doing of services for her brought so much peace. This is my reverend father, he said, suddenly despising himself for being noble.

Next morning came a letter. 'My dear Adrian, I am in Paris. From my room I see into the Luxembourg Gardens. There are children and donkeys. It is rather expensive, but my thoughts are such that I need comfortable surroundings and this view. I came here to be alone. Thank you for your marvellous letter. I shall answer it some day. Meanwhile I am very sad. Please write again soon. Linet.'

She rose before him, in great simplicity. There she was to his eyes in her pale blue shirt and pleated skirt; he could have patted her graceful shoulder, stroked the honey-coloured hair that was sometimes green. Why was she sad? What thoughts had she? How long before she would let him see her? It did not matter how long, for he was sure of Linet. Something in her letter spoke to the being within him that knew destiny. Adrian rested with that. He worked while the days lengthened; his thoughts took shape during the waking spaces of dreamy nights and grew while he slept. He worked all through a religious waiting-time, contented to stop now and then and repeat her name, quite certain the world would last till they came together.

HER second letter came when the roads were heavy with lilac and laburnum: 'Paris is delightful just now. The trees are new. I would be glad if it were possible to share it with someone — I will say, with you, Adrian. I have been into the country and picked flowers. There are some beside me now on the table. Do you think two people can ever make things perfect between them? Or do you think it would be wicked for two people who had known one extraordinary minute to risk spoiling it? It would be ruinous to spoil a thing like that with quarrels, or some meanness that people come to. With love, Linet.'

With love. Adrian felt that those words meant very much, from Linet. She wrote at critical stages in the movement of her thoughts with regard to him. It would not to do hurry her; he refrained himself, therefore, from going to Paris, though with difficulty. But he wrote that he loved her and felt himself capable of conduct that should do no injury to the past. After a few more days, on a morning of sullen and tremendous clouds, he received her third letter: 'There have been many days when I walked in the Luxembourg Gardens and looked at all the sweet children and their so devoted attendants, and felt I could pass the rest of my life here disembodied, looking and enjoying.

But I had a moment yesterday, in the Gardens, when I saw clearly that one must not be a coward. So let us try and deal with our friendship.' She added afterwards, in different ink: 'Mind you, I despise people who ask too much of things.'

He telegraphed: 'May I come?' She replied: 'I should like you to.'

He went that afternoon by the four o'clock train. There was no misgiving in him, no question this time of a journey into the unknown, the inimical; he was going to Linet, in perfect singleness and self-containment, with nothing in his will but the desire to see her, to hear her, to have her once more for his companion. It was stormy in the Channel, and France lay ahead across tossing seas under a weight of clouds; but Adrian dreamed on while the ship plunged and staggered, and Linet seemed to be with him, slight, mysterious, daisy-fresh. The train was late. Adrian stood in the corridor the last half-hour, and saw the illumination on the Eiffel Tower and the spectral shape of the Sacré Cœur. It was nearly midnight when they clanked into the station. Linet was waiting for him, without coat or hat, brushed and bright in those grimy surroundings, the very girl he had kissed in the glass-house. She gave a little mouse-like smile. 'I thought you'd like me to meet you.'

'It's wonderful to be met,' he said. 'Where are we going?'

'I booked you a room in my hotel. I thought you wouldn't have had time to book anywhere, or you'd

have forgotten. You must have a good sleep to-
night, and then we'll enjoy Paris to-morrow. It'll
be fun walking about with you.'

'Do you love Paris?' he asked.

'Yes, I lived here a long time. It's my home, in
a way.'

They drove across Paris in a taxi. Adrian's eyes
took note of the Louvre palace, the gardens, the
river; but he attended to nothing save the reality
that she was there beside him, fragrant and affectionate. It was a different Linet in some way. She
had been changed by some experience.

'Your eyes are luminous,' she said, 'and your
face has a look. Really, you're not unlike one of
your own sages.' He understood that they both
shone with the same light.

'I don't feel very removed from the world,' he
said. 'At least, I feel as if it didn't exist, as if
nothing existed but you and me. Nevertheless I
remain human.'

'I'm glad to hear it,' she answered. 'One wouldn't
want to go about with a ghost.'

The cab stopped. 'Here we are,' Linet said. It
was an hotel, narrow and high. 'It's no Ritz,' she
told him. 'Much better.' Across the road there
were railings and trees and a gloom of gardens.
Adrian could distinguish statuary in the shadows.
But Linet pulled at his sleeve. 'Come on. You can
look at everything to-morrow.' She led him into
the hotel, introduced him to a sour and upright
looking woman behind the counter, took his key

and her own, and put him in the lift. The lift went up tentatively, and they had time for conversation. 'She's hateful, that woman,' Linet said; 'but the proprietor is nice, and he likes me. This is our floor. And this is your room. May I stay while you unpack?'

He said 'yes, indeed'; and she stayed a few minutes and laughed at his packing, which in point of fact was very neat. When everything had been put away she solemnly shook hands with him and said 'good night.'

ADRIAN sat alone in the tower. He found it
scarcely possible to believe that those days of intense
living were in the past. It was all here with him
now, to live every minute again at will, as if time
had identified him with an experience, and left
him behind.

He was the prisoner of his memory, of certain
events and scenes that had so much more than
common reality, certain moments too sharp to be
believed. The experience had examined him in all
his capacities, and he might have taken pride in
achievement. He began to be conscious, indeed,
at this time, of new powers. It began when there
was evidence that he could obtain the attention of so
rare an individual. The reception of his work had
never given him such reassurance. Linet herself,
an observant, critical and instructed person, admitted his sensitive and adroit handling. But he had
all the humility of a lover, and ascribed everything
to her.

Curiously, that first night in Paris, when he
turned out the light and the striped wallpaper faded
into blackness, and ghostly trees in the Luxembourg
Gardens began to frame themselves in the window,
the old terrifying question asked itself loudly in his
mind, what am I, and where? He could dismiss
that question in familiar surroundings where his

eyes were able to recognize the shapes of the room; but here all was unknown. Except Linet; and it was strangest of all that he should be here with Linet, in another life. Linet herself was lying beside him, on the other side of the wall, in the same bed but for this partition; and there was a door between their two rooms. But it would be cowardly to knock, and useless, for there was still another partition between them invisible and impassable, and the door was shut by an unseen hand. She seemed to recede from him, with all else, and he was left to cope with this queer dissolution and un-namable terror alone. There was nothing for it, he knew, but to lie as still as he could with palpitating heart and dizzy head till that strange faintness of the personality died into sleep. Looking back, as he looked back now, such hours were inexplicable; it was absurd that such a thing should happen and such terrors gain any hold. There had been queer dreams, he remembered, and a rattling, and magical sunlight, and Linet or some fairy in an amber dressing-gown at the foot of his bed.

She had not floated in through the window with the warmth and sunshine; she had come by the door, now open between them. 'It's half past seven,' she said. 'I've turned on your bath.'

'That's friendly,' he said, believing himself to have died in the night and entered into everlasting spring.

'It must be nearly ready,' said the enchanting personality in the dressing-gown. She went into the bathroom to look, and he observed that she was wearing apricot pyjamas and green shoes. The sound of flowing water ceased.

Nothing of those unearthly minutes, her voice, her gestures, her look, the gliding of her sun-gilded form, the scent she brought into the room as if she were a flower, had faded or would ever fade from his memory. She tossed him a bunch of violets, and he was left to enjoy his bath in a kind of amazement. To his senses it was lapping lakewater, and he floated among opening lotuses, and sweet airs breathed from emerald mountain-tops. There was a kind of wildness and despair in him too, for the beauty of the world, for the miracle of Linet, for hints of a beatitude so much more than it was in him, or in man, to possess. Should he ever see her again, indeed, now she had gone through that door? Yet presently, at her summons, he went through the door himself; and there was her room in which she had been sad, a room tidy and delicious with flowers; there was Linet, lacing her shoes and faintly cursing.

But though in hand she was not yet his; though they walked about the streets and down by the river arm-in-arm, Linet hatless, she was remote from him, like thoughts and visions half seen and never yet captured. For the moment it was enough; it was difficult for Adrian to believe that even this privilege could be, to walk by the Seine with her hand in his arm and rout among the bookstalls; at present, he wanted no more. It was without his sanction, as it were, that the deep will in him reconnoitred her defences and engaged with the resistances it seemed to feel, as for instance when she refused, without reason assigned, to walk with him in the Luxembourg Gardens. 'Not yet,' she said; and there was wonder and sadness in her eyes that he pressed her — wonder and sadness and even pity, he thought. He understood there was some blindness in himself.

His blindness seemed strange in recollection, with the knowledge of what passed afterwards; though still, he reflected, silent in his tower, his knowledge of her was but little, and still he could not see clearly because of a cloud in his eyes.

In vision he followed those two figures through the streets of Paris, so deep in conversation, so absorbed in one another, that all the world knew their state and everyone but Adrian knew fully what Linet's mind was towards him. They found themselves in front of the Gare de Lyon. 'One goes to Italy from there,' said she. 'There's no journey more exciting. I shall never forget the first time — it was for my honeymoon.'

There is a state of happiness which nothing that has been in the past can affect. It was so with Adrian now; no jealousy darkened him, and he saluted her honesty.

'Italy is too beautiful to be quarrelsome and mean in,' Linet said. 'Another time I shall go there alone.'

There were many sad implications in this, and

73

now Adrian was perplexed. She saw the change in his eyes, and smiled, but he could not see what her smile meant. 'I see I must take you to the Luxembourg and explain myself,' she said next. 'You will probably have your way whatever happens.'

He had no answer until they came to a flower-stall. There be bought her a sheaf of narcissus. 'Because of some likeness between them and you,' he said, 'you shining slip.'

They had lunch in the sunshine at a table behind some shrubs, and Adrian watched while Linet attacked a Châteaubriant, underdone, with water-cress, peas and white wine from a carafe. 'Well, I've walked a long way,' she protested to his amused eyes. 'I'm not a fairy.'

He made love to her with his words, and her mood warmed a little; but her soul fled away once more when they reached the Luxembourg Gardens. They sat there a long time, beside a lawn, staring down vistas under a green ceiling between the ranks of black tree-trunks. There was a terminal bust among shrubs, birds hopped on the lawn, and sombrely clothed women devoted themselves to tiny children. Not far away, in an open space among the trees, a bearded priest organized a noisy game for some boys. They were silent, Linet and Adrian; they sat like birds meditating at the edge of the shrubbery, looking about them at views of lawn and path under the bird-haunted firmament of leaves. The gardens were drenched in sunlight, and there was much gaiety of flowers and children; but there fell on Adrian a deep afternoon sadness, as if behind the sunlight and the masses of foliage he detected the presence of some brooding and melancholy spirit.

'Are you happy?' he asked, to break the spell of silence between them.

'I think so. At least I wish this would never end, this afternoon. I wish there was no future. I feel like an insect among leaves, on a warm branch.'

'You are insect-like, in a way. A stick-insect.'

'Thank you!' She smiled. But was she not also very much a girl! How gracefully she sat! How the sunlight warmed her hair!

'Perhaps we shall have two or three afternoons like this,' he said. 'Though you always say one should never try to repeat experiences. I suppose I agree. It's a kind of boredom, to do that. One should taste what every hour provides, no doubt, for its own sake.'

'How long will you be here?' she asked.

'Three or four days. Then I must go back. I'm bound by my work.'

She frowned; a tiny look of severity came in her mouth. There was a moment of animosity between them. 'I find it strange to hear. I wouldn't be bound by anything.'

'No?' It was young to say that, young and admirable.

'Of course, three days is long enough for love,' she said next.

'Oh!' He could not help a tone of dismay. But it was evident she had been a little offended. What could he say or do? His feelings powerfully took charge. 'Before God, I shall not find all my life long enough for my love of you!'

She looked away from him. 'One soon becomes unhappy.'

Suddenly there were tears in his eyes, to hear such a bitter thing from her. 'I don't believe it!' he exclaimed. 'It's not true, what you think and say. There is love that lasts.'

'I haven't found it,' she said, turning her face to him; and how should he be jealous or angry when there was such sweetness in her eyes? She was all spirit and truth; her body spoke it to him. And Linet, with wonder perceiving the tears on his eyelashes, suddenly kissed them. 'Oh dear,' she said, 'perhaps I wish I had known you before.'

'I love you,' he repeated. 'You, now and always, with all my being.' There was nothing else in his mind but the truth of that declaration.

Now her eyes brimmed as she looked at him. 'Have you any idea what it was that made me so sad here?'

'Some. Not much.'

'In many ways you're a simpleton,' she observed. 'I'll never tell you what it was, but perhaps one day you'll understand of yourself. You ought to, you know. At least, you ought to know what I mean when I repeat that a short while is long enough for love. Because you have other loyalties and

76

another fate. Some day you'll love another woman, more fit for what you'll become.'

'I shall not!' he protested, knowing indeed more of the quality of his love and his nature than she had yet tasted.

But she did not seem to listen. 'Or else,' she continued, 'you'll love some other thing. You won't be able to help it, and I shan't mind — if I still know you. Oh yes! I will admit it, I'm in love with you now.'

He would never forget the sound of those words, or the warmth of that afternoon among the dreaming trees, or the May night.

HE could see her now, a white figure wandering along the road in the June twilight. She stopped once to stare up into an evening-shadowed tree, and once to look round at something unseen, perhaps some gleam of the sunset visible to her gaze. He felt a certain despair. She was more elusive than any vision that he had tried to capture; she would die away now before his eyes like that lilac stain on the roofs opposite; it did not seem true that he had held that flower, that fairy, or believable that he should hold her again. You will lose her one day — it was like a whisper in the darkening room. His being began to cast about how it might prepare and fortify itself against loss.

She came in by the small door in the tower. Presently she was in the room, hot and dusty. 'I've only just got back,' she said. 'Can I have a bath?'

'Of course. Where did you go?'

'Sussex. On the Downs.'

'Were you happy?'

'More than that. It was marvellous to be alone, and I had many thoughts.' She said this as if her thoughts were still with her. Adrian wondered what they were, with misgiving. He remembered their conversation of that morning, when he had refused to spend the day with her in the country,

78

on the grounds that he must complete a drawing for the Rev. Eugene Pollock. Indeed the mood for it was strong in him that day, and certain realities outside the world had seemed to him more important, more absorbing, than anything human. She had shown resentment, some jealousy of his work. It had been almost a quarrel. Now he brooded over her looks, her silences, while she dreamt upstairs in the bath. Perhaps he had lost her already through obstinacy, through blindness. In future, if he had but the chance, he would give himself altogether to her wishes; she should have the whole of his will. His heart prayed for the future, and presently Linet came down with a towel round her middle and the rose that he had cut for her stuck in the front of it, like a savage.

From their bed they could see the moon, a glowing lotus in the lake of the sky, floating among cloud-islets. Adrian caressed her with the rose, and laid it in the valleys of her body. She reclined on a bank of moonlight, with closed eyes; or turned her lily-pale face to gaze at him, as if a flower gazed. It was mysterious to lie there; they were hung up nowhere, in a net of shadows. She sighed presently, and whispered, 'No woman could forget you.'

He exulted to have so fully obtained her; there was a change and movement in him, as of a plant putting out many leaves. Yet he listened in the ensuing silence with anxiety; for there had been grief in the superb happiness of her whisper.

The silence was long. The moon stood now in a corner of the window and its brightness had passed from the bed. Linet spoke: 'To-night was perfect. We must never accept less.'

'What then?'

'What then? It's obvious — we mustn't ask for anything more.'

He sprang out of bed and went to the window. There might be help in the serenity of the summer night, in all that marvellous beauty, if he could breathe it in. Presently he was able to begin a question: 'You mean. . . .?'

'Why must we talk of it? Why can't you accept it?'

'I can't!' Once more he turned to the trees, as if perhaps he might drown himself in their selflessness.

'You're distressed,' she said. 'Why?' It was strange that she could be cold with him, now. He was taken with anger, standing there in the window; and in the hot light of his anger saw what seemed terrible to him — the ferocious will to possess her utterly and deprive her youth of its desire for other experience. His head swam. 'There are dark things in me,' he said at last. And then: 'I wanted to marry you.'

Now there was silence on her part, and when suddenly she came pattering to him in the window he perceived that there had been some change. 'That you shall never do,' she said. 'I'm not marriageable, in any case.' But she had wept.

He held her close and stroked her. 'Your hands tell me so much,' she said.

'They'll never have anything to tell any other woman,' he answered.

'Perhaps. It's marvellous to hear it. But one day they may have nothing to tell me. I have an instinct for this, Adrian, just because I'm so much in love with you . . . Oh! There can't be an end now, because of this argument. But soon!'

He could make no replies, and now his mouth could not warm her; she was obstinate and absent as death. There was daybreak, a faint lightening among the flowers that grew by the bed, and Adrian stood in the window, motionless, speechless, while Linet dressed. Presently she went as she had come, in her white frock, wandering along the road, stopping to stare up into a tree or gaze at something far off, invisible to him.

THREE days later, on a clear hot morning, Adrian visited Mr. Pollock with Mark, to submit designs. They were invited to lunch. The clergyman lived near his church in a house among trees where St. John's Wood borders on Primrose Hill, whose tree-crowned summit they could see across stretches of grass where boys played cricket. The house was kept by the clergyman's sister, a woman of seventy with a blotched face and the name of Salome. Their melancholy host had been a great traveller, botanist, and insect-hunter: he had much to show, and there grew up in Adrian's mind forest-pictures and insect-pictures. 'I could do a series of windows of the primeval world,' he said at lunch, escaping suddenly from sadness and bewilderment. 'Some world where vegetables and insects had brought each other to perfection. One would make an inspired use of light. I would create a dim dripping world of tree-ferns and spore-plants; and a world of vivid broad-bladed water-plants with glittering beetles over a pool; and a sinister world of poisonous white-veined plants, and shiny green-plated insects with long subtle claws and frightful eyes.'

'That would be very queer,' said Salome. 'How do you like working with such a queer man?' She addressed Mark, who had not said anything since they sat down to lunch.

Mark gave an affectionate grin, baring his dagger-like teeth, and replied, 'He's all right.' Then he engulfed a shoal of whitebait, all but some few tails that were chopped off in the guillotine of his mouth.

'Mark has a wonderful touch for angels' faces,' said Adrian. 'I should think he could soon do very good insects. They haven't so much expression, of course; but I prefer them.'

'Some more bread-and-butter, if you please,' said Mr. Pollock, 'and just a little more red pepper. These are very good, Salome.' He sat with his napkin tucked into the clerical collar, and ate with attention. When the whitebait were all gone he folded his hands, with a deep sigh, and Adrian found himself confronting the strange vacancy of those pale eyes. 'I can't wait twenty years for my windows,' the clergyman said; 'but I should be glad if I could. In twenty years you will be remarkable, if you govern yourself. You are changing. You have begun to reflect. I detect some loss of a perhaps extravagant richness; but there emerges an essential form and hue of the imagination, a style, if I may so call it, that is properly you. Forgive an old useless clergyman; treat me with the contempt due to an ossified structure, if you like. But I would say that there is still some danger that you may fall into the æsthetic of painting. Stained windows are stained windows.'

'It is a danger, I know. I must pay still more attention to form. There are so many dangers and pitfalls for an artist. Sometimes I can hardly face the responsibility.'

'I don't think you need fear. Your genius will look after itself, if you use ordinary prudence in the conduct of life.'

'Still,' Adrian said, 'it's an alarming thing to have inside one, especially if it won't let you alone to live your own life.'

'It sometimes appears,' the clergyman observed, 'that our lives are not ours to live. I warn you, young man, that you must remain celibate. A man like you must not divide his allegiance. Is that your view, Mr. Scoby?'

Adrian could not be sure whether he observed a kind of sad wink. But the clergyman's words watered the growth of some ideas of his own. 'Mark lives no life of his own — in a sense,' he said. 'He knows all about Hittites and Asia Minor. Ancient things live in him, and it seems to be very satisfying.'

Under Mr. Pollock's questions Mark became quite eloquent, and Salome listened with polite incomprehension. Adrian sipped a good claret, and watched those three queer faces. That blotched and brainless old Miss Pollock was giving them an excellent lunch. Certainly her sad-faced brother ate well: while he listened to Mark his palate was conscious of the flavour of kidney. Adrian's palate was conscious of kidney too, even while, in the silence now allowed him, his heart cried out for Linet. Not a word had come from her; no answer

84

to his letter. Oh yes! she would return undoubtedly and fulfil his longing for her society and conversation; once again their bed would become lilies, and they would obtain unearthly knowledge. But was there always to be this threat of an end? What if Linet was right? No! He protested against her talk of an end; and against this absurd talk of celibacy!

Suddenly Adrian envied all those who lead peaceful lives. Mark, for example; Mark was fulfilled in a hobby; Mark could not be disintegrated by a girl. Enviable Mark! Linet was no more to him than a grasshopper. As to Salome — one supposed she had known emotion, but she seemed fulfilled with the housekeeping, and managing the servants, and looking after her brother. Bella was in command of her life, in spite of suffering. As for Mr. Pollock, it was impossible to think of his being disturbed by a Linet. They enjoyed a peace that Adrian must attain; and the clergyman had advised him to look for it in submission to the creative mind within him. He stared through the window in deep thought, hardly seeing the grass and the trees.

'Taste this Pont L'Eveque,' said his host. 'A friend brought it to me yesterday from Normandy. Yes, thank you, I will have some too, a very little.' He sighed bitterly and shook his head, seeming to grieve over lost flavours. 'We can only have one thing at the expense of another.'

Coffee was brought, and a very nice glass of

85

brandy. Salome left them. Mr. Pollock and Mark were talking hard, but Adrian did not join in. There would be satisfaction in making that world he had seen, a world of unpassionate plants and unemotional insects. It created itself to his eyes now, in scene after scene — a frondy glade in the fern-forest, with some bright bug displayed on a stalk; battles among giant flies in dusty thickets; a tropic pool and the mating of fantastic beetles on the wet leaves of water-plants. Oh certainly, there were infinite complexities of light and pattern. One could achieve a desirable union of richness and form. Oh yes, and sometimes the burning imagination would be allowed to satisfy itself in some orchid. And chastened love might give its hue to the water-lily.

WITHIN a week Adrian was going across France with Linet in a train. The Mansfields wrote that they had taken a château in the neighbourhood of the Loire — not one of the big ones, it was explained; nevertheless, an historic house, a piece of rare beauty — and they would be glad if Adrian would visit them: they had asked Linet.

There was something peculiar in the situation, and Adrian was perplexed. But even before he had made up his mind to telephone, Linet came round in excitement and settled things. 'I'm terribly poor,' she said, 'I shall have to go by Dieppe.'

There was perhaps hesitation in his manner. 'You're coming, aren't you?' she asked. It was almost as if there had never been anything between them.

'I hadn't been sure if you would accept,' he said.

'Not accept?' Her astonishment was comic. 'Not accept?'

'And we shall go together?' Adrian did not quite know why he asked this question.

'But of course.'

They went, that evening. She had a heavenly simplicity. She was like a child about the holiday, in her impatience to start, in her excitement over the journey, in her copious and accomplished weaving of pictures about the château, the country,

the enjoyments there would be. She was like a
child about their passion. It was an important
discovery for Adrian that the pervading and
heavenly simple fact for her was that they were
lovers.

The evening was fine, and because of some warm
light on the downs, some splendour in the sky,
some note of beautiful desolation in the foreshore
beyond the quays, because all this touched their
communing hearts at the same instant, they passed
the night in a great ghostly hotel by the station.
It was a queer experience, after dinner in an
old-fashioned, empty dining-room, to stumble over
railway-sidings and between trucks, and stand
with their arms round each other, and stare at
spectral cargo boats gliding by on the river; to
return to their large comfortable room with its
long windows and curtains and Venetian blinds,
and its enormous bed. Their unsought experience
in this old-fashioned, dingy, and removed world
was strange and satisfying; the communion between
them was complete.

Linet seemed to remember something after she
had fallen asleep. She woke and turned to him.
'I suppose you'll be going back to your work in
two or three days.'

'We'll see. Perhaps not.'

'You'll go away with me, but you won't stay
away with me,' she said. 'I love your dark face
looking down.' She turned to her pillow and slept.

Next day there was rough weather, but they

crossed. Linet was very sick, and it was a be-
draggled figure that crept up the gangway and
climbed into the train. She reminded him of a cat
that has been out in the wet. She was only just alive
enough to protest when he pushed her into a
first class carriage and paid the supplement.

And now, after a night's rest in Paris, they were at
lunch in the train, on their way to Saumur. Linet,
perfectly recovered, was eating tournedos with
appetite. As they ran into Chartres he pointed
out to her the long roof and dissimilar towers of
the cathedral. 'We must go there one day,' he said.
'It's tremendous. You'll know then what windows
have been. And I shall show you what they are
going to be.'

She smiled at him. 'I like you to say things like
that. You take pleasure in your own powers, don't
you?' She reflected. 'You are very modest, though.
When you say things like that it's with a sort of
diffident temerity, and your eyes look shy. You are
entirely charming.'

He flushed under her praise. 'I feel always as if
the powers weren't mine,' he began.

But she was thinking of something else. 'It'll be
funny to be separated,' she said, with a cloud on her.

'We shall have to be?'

'Yes. While we are there. Perhaps I shall get
used to it. It may be beneficial.'

'It may be,' he said, 'because I shall teach you
what strong friendliness there is in our love.' She
gazed at him with bright eyes. 'There will be a

river, flowing and reedy,' he said, 'and vineyards, woods, and rich country, and I shall adore you. There'll be perfect friendliness between us: something indestructible. It will hardly even be necessary to speak, as long as we are often together, among those people. . . .'

'I don't know that I shall be contented with that,' she said. 'That country will miss something if you don't kiss me in it.' He was surprised to see big tears spurt from her eyelids and fall on the plate. She wept a little to think he was so high in love with her.

At Saumur they were met by Viola and Marigold, with Andrew, in a big car. The two young women showed delight in Linet, and Andrew — the capable, strong-browed Andrew — displayed a kind of earnest affection. Adrian, too, was received with evident pleasure.

'The journey must have been awful in this heat!' Marigold exclaimed.

'Thank you, parts of it were very enjoyable,' Linet said demurely. 'It was exciting to get the invitation. Is the château lovely?'

'Incredibly!' said Marigold. 'All Henri Deux and that, with initials everywhere. I can crawl out of my bedroom window into a lake.'

'There are fish a yard long in the river,' said her sister. 'You can see them where it's shallow.'

'Well, shall we get along?' proposed Andrew. 'I've stowed the suit-cases.'

Linet was put between the two girls on the back

seat, and Adrian sat in front beside Andrew. Presently they had crossed the bridges and were moving at high speed along the right bank of the Loire. It was pleasant beyond words to be in this company; but Adrian would have liked a few moments of solitude, to contemplate those shining reaches, the bright shallows and stretches of sand, the islets, the vineyards, the wooded hills and clustering villages on the further bank, the clear light that shines over that wide, that gracious river. Once he turned round to see if Linet was moved. Her eyes said, Yes, but I'm stuck between these chattering girls.

After a time they crossed the Loire and followed a tributary stream.

'There are troglodytes in those caves,' Viola told them. 'There's an awful hunchbacked one in our village. They tell us he's very wicked. An incarnation of the Devil, one old man said. They tried to drown him once, but he wouldn't go down.'

'Here's the village,' said Andrew. 'It's called Faye la Vineuse.' He turned into a cobbled, tree-shaded square, drew up before tall gates and sounded his horn.

Adrian began to take in glimpses of old roofs and walls, great-leaved plane trees, foliage and flowers luxuriant in the heat and splendour of August. Was he really to be here with Linet in this old, tranquil place? The gates were opened by an unshaved, polite man in leggings, and there was disclosed a view of the château itself, surprising and confounding in its perfection like music. The car should have been a coach, to fit that gravel drive, that perspective of lawn, fountain and radiating path. The drive crossed a fast-flowing river by a well-conceived bridge, and on the right hand there was a glimpse of antique houses coming down to the river's edge and villagers fishing. The car circled on the gravel and drew up at a front-door surmounted by the crown and sala-manders of a French king. In a moment Mans-fields were gathering from all sides to greet them; one, even, in a perambulator. Just a glimpse Adrian had of a lake and woods beyond and a hot evening sky. To be here with Linet! The perfection of that house had so engaged him that he had forgotten to seek her eyes.

Linet was seized and smothered by enthusiastic children. Mr. and Mrs. Mansfield gave Adrian warm greetings. They included a guest in their own self-interest, without prescribing too much for his activities. It was confusing, of course, to meet so many people, and hear so many names — Pam, Una, Michel, Mick (the youngest, the baby) Simone, Frances, Bob, Jerome, Selena. But they seemed well disposed; the younger ones, especially, regarded him with an engaging curiosity. They were not all Mansfields: Michel and Simone were French, brother and sister, elegant, grown-up young people. Simone, distinguishable from the other girls by her more self-conscious attire, dark-eyed and deliberate in her beautiful attitudes, was quite exciting. Her brother had something of the same quality; and Adrian was astonished at the heat of jealousy that rose in him when he saw Michel look at Linet and Linet return his look with accomplished self-possession. But it was absurd if he must waste time protecting his peace against so primitive a disturbance.

A footman came out for the baggage. 'Good evening, Richmond,' said Linet. 'Good evening, my lady,' the footman replied, and Adrian was astonished.

'It's not one of the big châteaux, as you see,' Mr. Mansfield explained. It seemed big enough to Adrian. They were in a comfortable salon, with a huge, painted chimney-piece, a mixture of modern and historic furniture, and a gilt monogram rhythmically disposed on the green leather walls. Through the windows, that held coats of arms in stained glass, one saw the sweeping approaches to the château. 'Henri Deux was here,' Mr. Mansfield said, 'and Diane de Poitiers, and Louis Quatorze. Mary Stuart visited here too. Linet has Diane's room, I believe.'

Mr. Mansfield's own man came to show Adrian his room and unpack for him. It was a small brown-hued room with gold in the wall-paper on the ground level. A great bunch of flowers had been set in the small window. The room was glorious with August evening. Adrian looked out while the man unpacked, and saw that the lake swept round here and he could crawl through the

93

window, drop on to some mossy steps and plunge into deep water. On his left was the perfect profile of a corner turret. From the scuffling he judged that two of the boys occupied the room next to him on the right. Beyond that Viola's head was thrust out of her window; she smiled at him. Beyond her a second turret, and a gleam of evening on the water, and trees darkening the bank. Where was Linet? They seemed to have taken her away.

But there she was at dinner, in a beautiful frock, and his heart sank; her elegance seemed to remove her. It couldn't be true that he had held that fashionable young woman, and there seemed no hope of it now. She chatted in French with that Michel d'Annecy . . . it became necessary to regulate his emotions. But when suddenly she gave him one acknowledging glance, to be here – to be dining in this magnificent room under that remarkable ceiling, panelled and gilded with lilies; to watch the light of evening change on the river and woods beyond it; to be one of this charming, this angelic company — seemed more than to be in this world. He succeeded in setting the Mansfields out in their order. Andrew, Marigold, Viola, Bob, Frances, Una — these six were at the dinner table. Jerome, Selena and Mick the baby were too young. They were without exception pleasing in their conversation and appearance. There was fine glass on the table, with a reflection of the river and evening woods in it. Viola's voice claimed him.

He turned to her and caught a glance from Simone, friendly, interested. He engaged in conversation with her across the table, and with Marigold. All these girls seemed contented with his society, and Mrs. Mansfield encouraged the talk. Really, there could be nothing more elegant than this civilized exchange, this unpassionate intercourse.

What satisfactions! What comeliness! Mr. and Mrs. Mansfield seemed contented with their life and their children; they lived as they thought it well to live, and hid no longings for other experience. It would be well for Adrian to live like this, married to Linet, getting her with children, dispensing hospitality, solid, confident.

After dinner they walked on the terrace, or watched the last light of sunset and their own reflections in the lake; and presently they drifted in twos and threes into the park. But Linet would not be alone with Adrian. He walked in the grass with his host and hostess, discoursing with judgment (for he liked to stand with people as a man of balance) on this and that, watching Linet who was twined up with Frances and Una, reflecting with an access of passion that this neglect of him was more severe than the circumstances demanded.

He despised himself when presently she came up and gave him her conversation, and he suffered again when she said good night without any promise of some moment at least for the exchange of their impressions. When all was silent he made his way back to the terrace, skirted the lake and found a seat under trees where he could watch the château, orange-painted in the glare of the moon. It was pleasant to sit there in the heat; he paused in his thoughts to admire the shimmer of his green silk pyjamas. That was Diane's room, where Linet slept. He thought of her now in Diane's bed, a woman somewhat more than mortal, like Diane herself. It was presumptuous to hope that she might be wishing for Adrian as she lay in her bed. But he had the recollection of her low surrendering voice.

It was worse than death if her desire for him should ever cease. And it was necessary that he should free himself from such fear. His thoughts whirled and he rose and began to walk up and down in face of the château. He glanced at it from time to time, and stopped in his walk to look more attentively.

His mind cooled. That jewel glowing in the moon, that symmetry of wall space, course and profile, steep-pitched roof and dormer window, exquisitely destroyed and completed with some perfect flaw, allayed his fever. He saw that it would be possible to obtain composure in the contemplation of that house, composure and indestructible delight. He tried to obtain it, with a measure of success.

ADRIAN had to employ the consolation of perfect architecture many times during the first part of their visit. Linet was friendly but not loving. Disposed by nature to a kind of sulky despair, and knowing it, he submitted himself to a discipline of sociability and good form. It was difficult. They were in an August heaven of rich river country, fine châteaux, and smiling friends; but each magical aspect of a meadow, each view of steep roof and dormer window seen over the trees, each sudden peaceful glimpse of hamlet and river, was altered, shadowed, ruined for him by her mood. They had tennis parties; they went shopping in Saumur and Angers; they played hide-and-seek all over the château; they rode, they swam, or lay in the streaming river on hot afternoons; they visited Amboise, Chenonceaux, Loches, Azay-le-Rideau, Chinon, and drank the wines of Touraine and Anjou in the vineyards of their provenance; but it would have been better for Adrian if Linet had taken his hand on some dungeon staircase, or given him her glass under the vines at Vouvray, or shared with him the rock where she lay basking in the river, or kissed him, perhaps, in the woods. Instead, she seemed less friendly with him than with the others; if she went alone with anyone it would

be Michel, or Andrew. If he pressed for it she gave
some formal reassurance, a tranquil kiss.

'Linet,' he entreated one evening, meeting her
in the stables. 'Has anything happened?'

'All sorts of things,' she replied.

'What? Have you . . . changed?'

'Everything changes.' She was cold, even as if
she had in her some dislike of him. 'I shouldn't
bother about it,' she added. She was removed, as
she would surely be when she fell out of love
with him some day. 'What else can I do here?' she
asked; and he might have read something from
that. He did not press her again, but swam and
rode and talked (though conversation was always
for him the most difficult of exercises) with the
others; and suffered abominably. He found a little
comfort in the particular friendliness of Viola; and
Mr. Mansfield, he fancied, watched what was
going on with sympathy.

There were moments when he seemed to perceive,
in contemplation of the château, something in
which a man might lose all griefs; but Linet
prevented him from that cold attainment by the
collapse of her mood and an outpouring of strange
indescribable griefs of her own.

They had ridden one morning, ten of them, to a
hamlet some miles away on the banks of the Indre.
The stream wound among poplar and willow, the
vineyards were rich, the sun cast deep shadows
in the angles of white cottages; they spread lunch on
the grass and made a picnic. A number of natives

were fishing — there was always leisure for fishing in that country: the scene was tranquil, idyllic. It seemed to Adrian there could be nothing more agreeable in heaven than to live among these fields for ever with that girl. There she was, sitting on a big stone, eating a pear. I love your slim knees, he thought, and suffered through longing. 'Will you come and fish?' he asked presently. 'We can easily get tackle.'

'I can't think of any sillier occupation,' she said.

He looked away, and the landscape seemed to have no colour. 'I'll come,' said Viola's soft voice: 'I like it.'

'Come off it, Linet,' said Andrew. 'Let's all fish.'

'Let's make her,' said Michel, and those two lifted and carried her, struggling and laughing, to a punt. 'We'll borrow it,' Andrew said. 'Bob and I will rake the village for stuff while you keep guard over her.' Adrian went with them. It was difficult not to give way to misery, and he found it necessary, when the tackle had been collected, to remove himself from the sight of her and take his punt round three or four bends in the river. Viola and Frances were with him: charming company. What could have been pleasanter, but for this poison in the mind? With a slight alteration in circumstances, what greater happiness than to spend an afternoon fishing, in this tranquil rich scene, in the company of these girls, Viola so virgin-mysterious, the younger Frances so enchanting in her excitement?

He watched Viola's dark brown head and her slim brown arms and hands: it was delightful to see her manipulate the rod. Oh yes — one must have a sense of proportion: this was but temporary with Linet; it was utterly wicked of him to have no faith. He talked with the two girls, therefore, and helped Frances to land a roach, and began to congratulate himself on self-conquest until sudden longing hurt his heart like a cramp. Damn it, it was absurd to be liable to such pain!

There was a splash upstream. Linet and Marigold swam past like otters. 'It is hot, isn't it?' said Frances. She looked at Adrian. 'Have we had enough fishing do you think, or would you like to go on?' Adrian smiled: her politeness was delightful. 'Let's take in our hooks and swim.' In two minutes both girls were pulling off their frocks; the foundation of their attire in that country was a bathing suit. They went over the side and Adrian, likewise prepared, presently went after them.

Without being able to help it, he sought out Linet and found her pretending some game under the roots of a willow. 'Hullo,' he said.

Her eyes looked at him across the water. 'I'd rather you didn't follow me about,' she replied.

It was astonishing. 'You're a perfect beast,' he said, and swam away, extremely surprised at himself.

Riding home late in the afternoon, he made up his mind to leave. Linet had been right: they should have parted before love came to this. But

how green and golden the afternoon! They should
have been riding together in the deep meadows
. . . and he must go, with this bitter memory
to eat away all others. The press of emotion was
unendurable; his chest seemed about to burst.
Here was a gate. He looked up. A horse jostled
his — it was Viola's. He held open the gate and
Viola, as she passed through, looked him in
the eyes. He rode on beside her, suffering discomfort with what there was of his mind and
emotions unabsorbed by the major grief. How
awkward! How sad, because . . . he gave the
matter a little more attention. A little exciting,
possibly. But it was merely Viola's way of saying
thank you. Yet he could not mistake the significance of that look; he had seen it in Linet . . . Oh
Linet!

He sought out Mrs. Mansfield. She was in that
little room with a view of the river through small
panes where Mary Stuart had liked to spend afternoons. 'Well, Adrian,' she said, 'have you everything
that is necessary to your happiness'?

'Not everything,' he replied. He was aware of
her scrutiny. 'It's absurd to be anything but happy,'
he said, 'in this lovely place.'

'Isn't it? But people will find the means anywhere.'

'You and your husband have the secret of
contentment. You live comely lives.'

'We are lucky.' Her smile was quiet, and for the
moment there seemed to Adrian nothing desirable

except a life of such richness and peace with some tranquil mate.

'I wonder if you've given your peace to your daughters.'

'My daughters?' She raised an eyebrow. 'Do you want one of my daughters?'

'No.' He met her eyes. 'I can't explain my trouble. It's nothing, after all.'

'Quite,' she replied. 'At any rate, you had better bite on it. You will have what is yours without worrying.'

'I'm sure that is so. Thank you.' She smiled again and he left her, without having said that he must return to London. He hadn't any idea whether she understood the situation.

It was a brilliant evening, golden and green. Adrian wandered into the grounds, seeking a retreat where he might be cool and reflect. Entering, he saw Linet under the vine leaves, face downwards on the seat with one hand over a lizard that lived in the rocky wall of the arbour. He could see her green and gold irises as she peered through her fingers at the captive. At his shadow she twisted quicker than the lizard and was on her feet: 'Adrian.'

'This is purely accidental,' he said. 'I'm not following you.'

She started, and he could not make out the significance of her look. Suddenly big tears swam down her nose and spurted from her eyes. 'Linet!' She was in his arms, crying as if she would never stop. It seemed as if that strange hate that she had for him were painfully melting. He had no notion how to comfort her. Kissing her was no use. Making light of it was no use. 'I've never seen such big tears,' he said. 'They simply leap from your eyes, and wet me. Your mouth is quite salt with them.' She raised her tear-drenched face for a moment, and plunged it once more in his breast, and wept uncontrollably. She looked, and felt in his arms, like a small child. He kissed the crown of her head, and patted her shoulders and sides, and her little bottom; but it was of no avail. Adrian simply did not know how to cope. 'But what's the matter'? he urged. 'Why are you crying?'

She shook her head, and he held her for a long while. It was sweet to feel her slim body again, its complete surrender, even though in grief.

'You must stop,' he said.

She made no response, and he shook her. 'I have stopped,' she said, looking up.

'Well, you must dry your eyes. It's quite time to dress for dinner.'

'You always know the time. Is that what most interests you. Doesn't it matter that I'm miserable?'

He shook her. 'If you say things like that again to me I shall box your ears.'

'Do.' She broke from his arms. 'I deserve at least that.' Suddenly she put out a capable hand and gave herself a sounding blow on the head. 'There.'

Seeing she would do it again, he pinned her arms. 'You mustn't do that, Linet. Please. Do come in to dinner.'

'I look awful,' she said. 'I don't want any dinner.'
All at once she became soft with him. 'I can't
possibly come in for hours. I look awful, and I'm
simply drowned in misery. Don't bother, just leave
me.'

'I can't.'

'I say you are to. You're to go in and have your
dinner. Say I'm not well. Kiss me.'

She put up her grief-spoiled face. All his being
loved her. 'Come back afterwards,' she whispered
into his mouth.

At dinner Adrian explained that Linet did not
feel well. 'I know,' said Frances. 'She's in one of
her miseries, poor darling. I saw it beginning.'

Adrian caught a glance between Mr. and Mrs.
Mansfield. As for him, he was happy: was not
Linet somehow now more than ever his? After
dinner he escaped, and went to Linet's retreat
with some cake and fruit. She accepted agreeably.

'You are kind-hearted,' she said. 'You loved me
when I was crying.'

'I did.'

'You've got a good deal of woman in you.'

'You wouldn't say I was feminine?'

She laughed at his anxiety. 'No, Adrian, I
shouldn't. You are extremely male . . . as I've
good reason to know.'

'And you are completely girl,' he told her, 'although you live to quite an exceptional degree by
reason. Why did you cry'?

'It comes over me sometimes. I'm simply

swamped in misery. But there's always a cause. Suddenly I see what a failure I am. I've never brought anything off: not a single thing. My marriage . . . he was a beast to me, but he wouldn't have been if I'd been different, if I'd known better how to run things. . . .'

'That's a ridiculous argument,' Adrian broke in.

'It isn't. It's true. I try so many things and fail. Will you ever forget what I've been like to-day?'

'Will you ever forget my rudeness?'

'You weren't rude. I was simply horrible to you. You must have wanted to drown me.'

'I did.' All at once he saw how like a child she was. 'I should have liked to give you a smacking.'

'You shall, sometime,' she humbly said, and he promised himself that he would. Yes, like a child, living in a region of imaginative reality, living after all . . . well, living. As angels live, by heavenly values.

'Why have you been so cold this past week?' he asked her.

'Don't you understand?'

He shook his head.

'It's simple.' She took his head in her hands. 'I love your dark intent face. You looked so severe when you found me this evening, like a god that is minded to destroy someone. I should like to be destroyed by you.'

'You talk nonsense,' he said. 'But why were you so cold to me?'

'In some ways you are thick-headed, my dear.

Because of this dreadful passion, Adrian. I tried to
be as if I hadn't got it, because it's absurd to be in
love with anybody like I am. Stupid to try, perhaps.
I failed, anyhow.'

'Is that why you wept, because you failed?'

'No. I wept because of the passion.'

Her speech was like the rising of the moon. He
took her into his arms, and they sat silent under the
vine leaves.

IT was getting near the end of their stay. 'This week has been perfect,' Adrian said. 'We were so much one that we scarcely felt passion. God must be like that, possessing everything within Himself.'

She looked a little distrustfully. 'Would you wish it to be like that always between us?'

He suffered a change of mood. 'No! Oh no! It's like the time when I was first waiting for you. I said your name over and over to myself, and it was marvellous to wait for you: but it would have been agony if I hadn't begun to be sure that soon when I said your name you would be in my arms to hear me, and you would be my mistress.'

She smiled. 'I like to hear you talk that way. And are you sure of me at this moment? Are you certain I shall be your mistress again?'

'Perfectly certain.'

'Well,' she answered, 'you're right.'

One evening they were alone after dinner with Mr. Mansfield on the terrace. Linet was sylphine in a slight ivy-green frock, and Adrian filled his eyes and heart with her graceful figure. At the end of a silence during which he seemed to ponder deeply Mr. Mansfield said, 'I think you two ought to marry. There's a fate laid on you.'

Perhaps both of them, foreknowing, shuddered a little at his words. 'I will never marry,' said Linet.

'How can I? I'm married already. Funny that I don't even know where Carl is.'

Mr. Mansfield appreciated his cigar. 'I think we could soon find out. I've explained to you, Linet, that it would be quite possible to obtain a divorce, and I've offered to negotiate for you.'

Linet was obstinate. A little severe, scornful look that Adrian knew came into her face. 'It's all one to me. There's no point in being divorced. I shall never marry.'

Adrian would not urge her in Mr. Mansfield's presence. He stared at the moon rising over the park, and wondered if her will was against divorce because that would be the final end of a marriage from which she had hoped much, the last evidence of its failure — her failure, as she magnanimously conceived it.

'Well,' Mr. Mansfield asked, 'what is your future to be? What are you going to do about Adrian? Forgive me if I press you, but there is a sense in which you are made for each other.'

Linet wriggled. 'We'd better not spoil it then by marrying.'

'Have you no sense of compromise with reality?' Mr. Mansfield blandly enquired.

'Yes,' said Linet. An answer trembled on her tongue. She looked at Adrian for permission, and he nodded. 'We are lovers already,' she said. 'We compromised that way, before we came here.'

They both, Adrian knew, experienced the same delicious confusion. It seemed beautiful that anybody should know. Mr. Mansfield looked thoughtful. 'That's all right,' he said at last. 'But it's not in the long run a satisfactory way of dealing with things.'

'There won't be a long run,' Linet said, and Adrian felt irritation with what seemed unreasonable persistence.

'Oh yes, there will,' Mr. Mansfield replied. 'You can't help it. With people like you there must be — take my word for it. I don't know if Adrian thinks the same as you do?'

'No,' said Adrian.

'Well, the issue's important. It's foolish of me to have interfered, I expect. Better leave you to thrash it out.'

He left them, and both felt, Adrian knew, as if they had been married, as if he had blessed their marriage and left them to one another.

But Linet persisted, though with a kind of sob in her voice. 'I've wondered if we could ever be fools enough, criminals enough, to live together.'

'You must have suffered horribly,' he said, 'to make you say things like that.'

She was in his arms again, and again there were salt tears on his mouth. 'It would be wonderful if we could come here together and share the same room,' he whispered.

'All sanctioned and sacramental? You are profoundly conventional, Adrian.'

'As an artist, would you say?' He was suddenly alarmed and she laughed at him.

109

Then she too was alarmed. 'That's what means most to you, your art?'

'Not so much as to lie in Diane's bed with you.' He reflected. 'Linet . . .' He wondered how she would take this. 'You understand I must be going back soon. I can't be spared any longer.'

'Oh!' He perceived that faint estrangement and withdrawal. 'I suppose you could scarcely spare a few days with me in some village here.'

'I've hoped for it,' he answered.

A shout came from a window, and Linet swiftly gave him her hand. They were to join the others for a moonlight bathe in the lake. Presently moving dark heads were to be seen in the water, and silver heads in the moonroad, and figures diving from the terrace. Then there were sandwiches and lemonade in jugs. And in due course silence, and Adrian, from the further bank of the lake, watched the lights go out one by one. He saw Linet look out between her shutters, and when she had vanished he stared for a long time at the cavern that was Diane's room.

Iᴛ was the last day. Adrian sat in his bathing
suit on the parapet of the bridge, fishing in the
river, with an obedient Linet beside him. Andrew
was fishing from the bank, a little upstream. Marigold, Simone and Michel had disposed their limbs
in the grass until it should be time for a swim. Viola
was reading, or dreaming, under an elderberry
with Mick in a perambulator at hand. The other
children could be heard in the distance. A great
fish nosed in the water below, wilfully blind to the
inducements that Adrian held out. 'He's not
hungry,' said Linet. 'I would like to be a fish.'

'It's difficult to remember that they haven't got
any brains and can't be enjoying themselves,'
Adrian observed.

'I expect they do enjoy themselves, in some way.'

'There may be enjoyment in some sense,' he
agreed. 'They want to go on living, it seems.'

'I am enjoying myself,' Linet said. 'I would
like this to go on for ever.'

'I, too. What could be better than to continue,
so to speak, in this minute, holding all our recollections and anticipations?'

'I wonder how it would feel, though, if we weren't
really going to have to-morrow and be alone. For
us, there's always something better to come. So far
each one of our perfect minutes has been more

marvellous than the last. . . .' But this train of thought led where her mind was too familiar.

'There's no reason,' said Adrian, 'why with skill in self-management we shouldn't achieve an almost unearthly happiness.'

'We should have to pay for it,' Linet said. 'Look at your float.'

Adrian landed his fish, and Linet passed him a fresh worm.

'Don't you find her exciting?' Linet indicated with her thumb the elegant Simone.

'No,' said Adrian, who did not care much for dark women.

'I do,' Linet said. 'If I was a man I'd make love to that girl. I'd like to be a man. They have opportunity and initiative as well. . . .'

Adrian looked sideways at her. But Mick the baby began squalling: it was a signal to something restless in everyone. A nursemaid fetched Mick, Viola walked to the river-bank and looked towards the pair on the bridge, Andrew put up his rod, Marigold, Simone and Michel rose from their forms in the grass, children gathered from here and there. Adrian and Linet watched from the bridge, still in the spell of their happiness. Presently came two or three swimming, and faces peered up from the water. Linet swung herself over the parapet, hung by her hands a moment, and dropped into the water beside Michel whom she promptly ducked. He pursued her and she dived. Adrian watched their bodies turning like shadows down in the dark water under the bridge. He had no jealousy now.

Presently he swung himself down. It was delightful to lie in the soft-flowing shallow river, to nose along the bottom, or paddle upstream with the water flowing against your mouth. Adrian observed Viola still standing on the bank. 'Aren't you coming in?' he called, and was relieved that she responded with alacrity and swam beside him, or stood with her feet on the bottom, talking; it removed the little feeling of discomfort that he was apt to have in her company. If she felt any jealousy of Linet (and why on earth should she? Was it reasonable to presume she might desire him? Yet, if Linet, why not Viola?) she hid her feelings in a way he admired; and he was only dimly aware of tension.

In the afternoon everyone drowsed, because of the great heat, among trees, in vine-screened arbours, under the bushes in a punt. Everyone was a little melancholy, perhaps; for these were the last summer-laden hours, and already it was cool sometimes at night. Adrian lay on his bed in that brown-tinted room with gold in the walls, hands clasped under his head, staring at the flowers in the window, and the ivy and the deep leaf-light beyond. Why should any Mansfield be sad? They would soon be taking some other graceful pleasure. They were going to Scotland, in fact, for the autumn; and then perhaps to London until the winter-sports, and then perhaps . . . well, to some castle in Spain. And why should Adrian be sad, when to-morrow he should begin with Linet a time of solitude on the banks of the Vienne? It was strange that there should be any possibility of sadness, in these circumstances. Yet sad he was; merged, perhaps, through the stillness of his contemplation, in some vaster sadness or foreboding.

This mood continued, and Adrian sat as silent as he might be throughout the last dinner-party under that rich ceiling in the many-coloured room where a French monarch had been used to take dinner with the more than mortal Diane. Did she also sometimes sit there in a brown study, absorbed in those views of woodland and river, given up to incomprehensible imaginings, like Linet? He glanced across at Linet, who sent him a swift secret smile. He drew breath suddenly. To-morrow!

After dinner they danced until late. Linet and Adrian divided themselves amongst the others, separate for that last evening. Finally, when everyone else was in bed, Adrian walked all about the grounds by himself, visiting loved places – the stables and dairies, the bridge with its view of the sleeping village downstream, the flower gardens, the lake, each aspect of the living château. It stood there, pale in the starlight, as if it breathed, as if, rather, after all life of the body had ceased it had existence in heaven. Adrian thought not at this minute of anyone within the château; he thought only of that perfect shape, and knew himself to have received power.

Thus, when later he stood in the shadow of trees

by the pool, and saw a face at a window, and understood presently that it was Viola, and that she wept, it seemed strange to him for a moment that there should be place for grief in that mansion, and he looked at her coldly. Then in a minute he stepped out and reached up for her hand on the window-sill, and she saw him as if he came to her in a dream.

'Don't cry,' he whispered, and perhaps communicated through her finger tips some share of that consolation he had himself received.

THE night was moonless and scented. Through the wide-open window Adrian could see the thriving leaves of plane trees; he could hear voices in the square below; a little breeze wandered like a ghost in their large room. She reached out a hand and took a rose from the vase by the bed and drowned herself in the scent of the flower. Presently she turned her breast to him, and whispered 'You have my heart.' Her words filled him with terrible sweetness.

Not many nights were left. The day for departure had been agreed on, and Linet seemed to have dismissed all thought of it; she lived, Adrian too, so intensely in the present that the present seemed to have infinite extension, both ways, without memory of antecedents or intuition of things to come. Dear Linet! It pleased him especially to look after her, to have sole care of her, to afford shelter from what after all she must find an inimical world. She would not depend on him for the holiday — at the beginning she handed him her money and forgot about it; but she did seem for the time to rest in his presence, to relax and give herself up to the fact of him. She accompanied him by day, and lay in his arms by night, a well-protected child, ardent young woman, too, and mystery.

She wasn't playing with the rose now. She was

asleep. He stole to the window and sent thanks
starwards for the sweetness of that night with her.
There came to him a faint unpleasing memory
from the daytime. They had climbed up at
evening to the castle of Chinon to look far over river
and sunset country from the height of the battle-
ments. She stood in the crook of his arm, gazing
afield here and there, busy with unguessable
thoughts that had yet, he felt, to do with himself
and her. On the way down, in dusk, through the
ruins, they stood before a bare chimney-piece in the
remains of a room where Jeanne d'Arc was said to
have been and were startled to hear a voice. It
came from a small figure crouching there, and
they recognized it — the hunchback whom the
people of Faye la Vineuse had tried to drown. He
was not so much a hunchback. Adrian perceived —
there was simply something traditional and conventional of evil in that name — as a man wholly
deformed, or rather a man wholly lacking form,
through the lack of any centre of co-ordination, or
soul, or point where life might flow into him and
irrigate his nature. He jeered. He spoke, as far
as they could understand him, of love. He had a
contempt for the invariable symptoms and fatuous
yielding of lovers to typical illusions. It was amazing
what fantasies they could make with a little heat.
Better if people would recognize what moved them
and cool their heat sensibly. Adrian drew Linet
away. 'Tell your tales then,' the cripple shouted.
'You'll tell the same tales to another when you're

in the same state.' He followed them to the village, grinning as if he saw an obscene fact at the heart of all illusion. Changing for dinner they had been a little sober, at first; Adrian, indeed, felt a certain coldness and sinking of the heart, for he was reminded of a waiter who looked foully at him when he had said goodnight to her in that Barcelona hotel, reminded also of the answer that his own nature then produced, of old doubts, of something in himself that found truth in what the cripple alleged. But their intimacy in that room they shared was very real and convincing, and with dinner they forgot. Adrian was not quite sure, at moments, whether Linet had quite forgotten; whether perhaps she had not just put away her recollection of that scene in the ruins. But when they lay in their bed remembering each indescribable moment of their experience together, it was fully and warmly known to be of the spirit, and they felt awe in the possession of something indestructible, a gift out of heaven, a portion of immortal being. He felt a pang of fear suddenly, an old fear, and turned for reassurance of Linet. She slept. Her pyjamas still lay on the floor by the bed where he had dropped them, two pools of silk. He woke her enough to make her put them on, sleepy and sulky but obedient. She had said, 'You have my heart.'

ADRIAN lay in bed, pleasurably reflecting. The young person in lilac pyjamas had gone into the bathroom for her usual prolonged ablutions (two or three times a day Linet was to be found in the bath — soaping herself, Adrian said, unnecessarily). He smiled to hear her scrubbing her teeth and spitting. Impossible that this should be the last time! Imperative that she should live in his tower, and spit in his bathroom! He lay thinking out arguments, ways and means; and presently she came in.

'It's very much colder this morning,' he said.

She paused in her movements, frock in hand. 'Well, what of it?'

'You must wear more clothes. We shall be driving back to-night in an open car.'

Linet had on a cotton vest and a pair of cotton drawers. She laughed. 'I never wear more than this.'

'You must when I'm looking after you,' he said.

Linet made to put on her frock. He sprang out of bed and seized her. She was an armful to manage, strong and slippery as an eel; but he overcame and gave her a cautionary smack. 'Now will you do what you're told?'

'No.'

Adrian sufficiently redeemed a promise made to himself at the château. 'Now will you?' he asked.

She submitted, proving however with many arguments, while she added somewhat to her clothing, that it was all unnecessary and he was making an absurd fuss. 'I only agree to save time,' she said. 'You don't know how to spank,' she added. 'It ought to hurt much more, from what I remember.'

'I shall soon learn,' he said.

They went down to have breakfast in the café, at a little table on the pavement, with full survey of the square and the market stalls under the plane trees, and the sculptured church opposite.

There was another English couple in the hotel. They were having breakfast at the next table. 'Doesn't she look proud?' said Adrian, indicating the wife, a statuesque and well-groomed blonde. 'They never take any notice of us.'

'We don't mind,' said Linet. 'But if I was a man I'd have that proud, cold look off her face.'

'I'm sure you'd be irresistible as a youth. Though thank God you're a girl. I can see you devastating the female population. Pleasing them infinitely. . . .'

'I'd just see that face of hers changed with passion,' Linet said, 'and then I'd say, "Good-bye, and thank you for a nice afternoon".'

Adrian laughed. 'You're remorseless with your own sex.'

'I understand them. That's the way to be.

Send them away when you've done with them. I wouldn't have any woman clinging to me, loving me, claiming on me. . . .'

'Oh! . . . I don't feel like that. . . .'

She scanned his face for a minute and stroked him protectively. 'Nor do I, then. But I'm a woman, in this life.'

'To be as we are seems to me the summit of human felicity,' Adrian said. 'Really, I'm frightened at my own happiness. Are you?'

'Yes, I am.'

'It's simply unendurable this should be the last day,' he went on. 'Let's stop. Let's never go back. What does my work matter, after all, in comparison with actual living?'

He pleased Linet, but she showed a new mind. 'If anything matters, that does. Your work as an artist matters much more than your life or mine.'

After breakfast they drove in their hired automobile to Loches. Adrian wished to spend their last day revisiting the dungeons and torture-chambers of that grim castle. 'I hate tortures,' Linet said, 'but I was happy here that day, though you didn't know it. Happy looking at you. Not happy, perhaps. Perhaps sad. More than ever, because I knew that day that I couldn't help myself any more.'

Once again, therefore, they examined the vaulted chamber where the Cardinal was hung up eight years in a cage, the embrasure where the Duc d'Alençon was imprisoned, the dungeons, oubliettes and instruments of torture. The guide was eloquent; his interventions were swift, dramatic, disquieting when in the darkness of a lower dungeon he suddenly put out the candle. Linet compared his performance with the previous one, and could detect no variation. 'I like Louis Onze,' she said. 'Better than the later, more magnificent kings. He was sardonic, cruel — though I don't believe it can have been so bad as you might think to be hung up in a cage eight years. They let the Cardinal see people. And it must have been rather amusing, really, when Louis came in to vituperate. Still, there was that pit with the bar for breaking men's wrists. And all those things. One wouldn't have cared much about being brought in here through the gates, knowing what was inside.'

She lingered over the tomb of Agnes Sorel. They stood looking at the effigy with their arms round each other. 'I have a sympathy with women who were mistresses,' she said. Presently she added: 'All the best women were.'

'I wish you and I could lie side by side on a tomb in some old church,' Adrian said. 'It would be marvellously peaceful to be united for ever in that way.'

'I'd want to be able to turn to you sometimes,' she said.

He smiled. 'We would be surrounded, perhaps, by windows of mine; landscapes on either side, with the light in them that I've caught from your spirit; and our faces towards heaven and thronging angels, and Almighty God looking far beyond us. . . .'

They were silent, thinking of the great universe and their love.

In a mood, perhaps, for churches and tombs, they found themselves, towards afternoon, in the village of St. Denys where there is a church built partly in the fourteenth century. They went in, and sat down in the north transept where afternoon light poured on a great altar with a gilt screen and many images in shrines and a forest of candlesticks and flowers. To one side was the Virgin on a column with a sheaf of white roses and a lace veil and jewelled crown. Beyond, there were other chapels with flowers and images, and a soft light streamed from windows high up in the choir. Their own window in the transept shed heavenly radiance on altar and Virgin. They knelt, side by side. How innocent, how solemn, how blessed Linet looked! What long and heavenly thoughts had she? Adrian prayed for her with an anguish of the heart, prayed for her safety, her happiness, all foolish human goods, and the ultimate peace of her soul; knew also that she prayed in like manner for him. She gave him a little smile presently when her ecstasy was finished. They knelt while the light reddened and faded in the windows, and a little shiver of evening entered the church. They left then, with clasped hands, knowing that this was their marriage.

PART II

[- 1 -]

THREE of the Reverend Eugene Pollock's windows were in position, and a good many people had come to see them. It was a Saturday afternoon in May. The three windows were on the westward side of the library. The remaining windows, including the single window that occupied a great space in the south wall, were filled temporarily with opaque, greenish glass. The room was beautifully proportioned, with austerely moulded ceiling. The visitors moved in a sombre radiance, kaleidoscopic, insubstantial; they stared at the strange windows, or murmured in sea-green light. Some inspected the books on their oak shelves. Friends of the clergyman were there — wry, studious people of unconjecturable calling; connoisseurs from three or four capitals were there, and several of those wealthy, smart-like, high-talking people, exotic within what fashion allows, who flourish at such occasions and patronize them; the Mansfields were there; Linet was there, in a delphinium-blue frock, distinguished hat (which she held in her hand, shaking her hair free), and admirable shoes. There was much conversation and movement; but the main preoccupation was the windows. They affected people like a Presence. People said

125

they were sombre; there was a gloom in the heart of their effulgence; the figures were tremendous, brooding, and inhuman in their aloofness. That might be so, a few said, and they were glad of it: it was time people got knowledge of what was more than human again.

The occasion was less painful than usual for Adrian. There was here attainment that he had to recognize; there had come into the world a new grace, a new severity, a vision and presentation at once idiosyncratic and impersonal. He was aware of a sufficing isolation as he considered his work. A man from some German town offered him a steel church to decorate; a tall man in a stock proposed that he should make windows for a new house in Park Lane; he treated, but with an external activity that maintained and protected his contemplation. Those colours — that brown, that lilac, that ruby gloom — were themselves vision. They flowed from understanding, they matched experience. It was by guesses of his own experience that he perceived a mystery in the Annunciation, understood Gautama's renouncement, the blessedness of his release from desire. But Jehovah he had not loved; Adrian saw it suddenly. That window, splendid, thunderous and fierce, was a masterpiece of pattern; but there was more pattern than experience in it, and no life of his.

'I may destroy that one some day,' he said to the Reverend Mr. Pollock.

'It may destroy itself,' that gentleman mysteriously said. 'A work of art carries its own fate within itself, like a man.'

'I understand you,' said Adrian, on reflection.

The wall had been pierced between the tops of the windows to allow of small five-pointed flowers of colour required in the decoration, one over each bookcase. The clergyman considered these.

'I attach importance,' he went on, 'to those five-pointed flowers. I make use of analogy. It is with reverence that I say they resemble creations of the Almighty; they are whole, simple and affecting like some flower in His fields. They are also curiously yours, as if while you were making them you became what God particularly designed you to be. Have you understood yet, I wonder, the specific quality and true object of your genius?'

Adrian frowned. 'I don't know. Sometimes I am a little tired of it. I wish I might be let off. At the same time I don't know what people live for if it isn't their destiny to create. More than that. . . .' But Adrian checked his own fervour: he did not wish to speak of that experience of a perfect meaning and shape by which he had achieved a measure of self-containment in love. 'My mind,' he said, 'is bent chiefly on the window that I shall tackle last.'

Mr. Pollock raised his eyelids. 'I do not ask that I may live long enough to see it; but I can provide for it in my will. What is the subject?'

'The Tao.'

'When you understand that, my poor means of appreciation will have ceased to convey sensations.

127

'I am sorry,' said Adrian, 'but it is a necessity for me that I should understand that philosophy.'

'Then I suppose the world must wait for this window. I commiserate your wife. Am I to have the happiness of marrying you presently?' His expression would have saddened a funeral.

'I am not sure that Linet will be married in church,' Adrian said.

'She will need all the usages of religion,' the other replied. 'And ultimately, if I am not mistaken, the refuge of a convent.'

'I think you are mistaken,' Adrian was disturbed that Viola Mansfield listened and watched.

He went over to Linet, suddenly longing for her. 'I'm so glad you've come,' she said. 'I wanted you, and I couldn't be public, among all these people. How outside us they all are!'

She was sad to-day; in face, possibly, of something she perceived in his windows. Certainly this enchanting person was often sad in this world; and she mocked it, he perceived, because it was in fact somewhat harsh and gross for the sweetness and delicacy of her mind. But with what courage she made good her ideals in the world, living inflexibly by the light she perceived in heaven!

'I admire,' said Mr. Pollock, drifted against them by the crowd, 'the little window that is like a night-black pansy.'

'It's beautiful,' Linet agreed; and added, for Adrian's ears only, 'that's essentially you.'

'Surely I'm not so dark!'

'You are — pansy-dark. I've felt you were when I've been hidden in your arms at night. Oh, and your mind is so dark and secret!'

These words gave Adrian a kind of fright: he had thought himself open.

'Such mysterious processes are always going on in you,' she said. 'And then these strange windows appear. They are strange. There's something unreal in them that is more than real. The figures are gods and demons. They are what no other man would have made. And I'm never sure of the will in you, which way it's going — except towards one thing.'

'And what's that?'

'More windows.'

'Ah, no, Linet! Towards you, always.'

She smiled, negatively. It annoyed him when she wouldn't see what was so clear, that he loved her before all else; that if he knew anything, achieved anything, it was through and for her. He remembered that he had made a Madonna in her likeness before ever he saw her. 'Linet!' he whispered urgently, 'you are wholly beautiful in soul and body. You are more than ever I dreamed a girl could be when I was a youth with my head always on fire. You endlessly satisfy every desire of my nature. How could I tire of you when you're always new, always strange? How could I turn away when all else there is must be less?'

He felt pressure of her fingers, but she hid her eyes from him. A black pansy! He continued to reflect on it, staring at his own windows to see what it was in them that people found strange. Then Bella came up, in her usual black dress, only now able to be out again after a bout of illness. Adrian had done his utmost to help her through that, visiting her, reading to her, doing everything he could think of to alleviate her condition; but it was with effort, and as it were with some desire to abolish the fact of pain from the world, or at least to diminish it. It was a fact, though, that he must squarely contemplate some day; even, he felt with a chill of foreknowledge, profoundly experience. It was idle to have made these windows, presumptuous to have undertaken these themes, without having suffered in his own spirit the pain of the world. Yes, he would perhaps destroy them all some day. In the meantime he shrank from Bella, her haggard face, her martyred eyes, as if she were the prefiguration of his own agony.

'Well, Linet,' Bella said, 'this is a great day for Adrian.'

'It is indeed,' Linet replied.

'It is not Adrian who matters,' Mr. Pollock unexpectedly said, 'but something more. This is a great day, we might say, for some spirit, I know not what, that works continually.'

The two women conversed together. Adrian felt antagonism between them. Bella was kind to Linet: loved her, indeed; but she was critical with some strong part of her nature towards the woman who could become Adrian's mistress, or any man's.

Adrian had wished to bring Linet straight home with him — if she would come. Bella had in any case opposed it. 'Why can you not wait for each other?' she asked. 'You'll be married in a year or so. Meantime you have your love. Why must you live in what I'm afraid I must think of as sin?' There was a profound inexperience here, or so it seemed to Adrian, that he could not argue with. Certainly he would not do anything to give Bella embarrassment or (short of separating for so long from Linet) grief. But they had separated, because of arguments put forward by Mr. Mansfield's lawyer, at the inspiration, Adrian felt, of Mr. Mansfield himself. Linet had spent a few months in Belgium having charge of somebody's odious daughter, earning money for clothes; and Adrian had taken refuge from his longing in these windows, and in a project for those insect-windows and plant-windows that he would create some day when there was a place for them. Indeed, he worked powerfully in this state of tension. But twice, and at the same time, as if they had constant sight and immediate knowledge of each other, their passion waxed in such a way that each wrote to the other, desiring to meet; and taking all risks they met, in Antwerp. Sweet dangerous days! Adrian would not forget that high, luxurious room with its florid anteroom, and the great bath; mornings in the old printer's house, afternoons in that fabulous zoo, nights in that mysterious bed with Linet like a dream beside him. Oh yes, and they knelt on the

131

sofa by the great window, with their arms round each other, watching the people in the square. Was it true that this had happened, that a man had experienced such unearthly pleasure!

'An artist may have pity,' the clergyman was saying. 'He may even share people's sufferings with them; but it will be in the cause of his own transfiguration. He will weep to understand tears. . . .'

Adrian was suddenly furious with all this talk about artists. He was a man before all else, comforting Bella because he was sorry for her pain, taking care of Linet because he loved her like a child. His heart was moved with such love now, for was not her face sad? He understood her. How much more she was a woman than he had known at the beginning! He saw clearly that she feared the calm, the remoteness, the fierce pre-occupation of his Buddha with non-being. To-night, many miles from here on the Kentish coast, he would give her comfort for that.

[- 2 -]

'I DON'T really care for your house,' Linet said. 'I don't think I shall come and live with you after all.' She was squatting in the window-seat of Adrian's room in the tower. It was the Tuesday morning following the ceremony at Mr. Pollock's.

Adrian was alarmed at her words: he didn't know how much she meant them, or what irritation it was that they disguised.

'Couldn't we start now, instead of after lunch?' she enquired.

Adrian had known this question was coming. He bent over the plans and calculations on his table. There was hostility in her voice. One must be careful. 'I'm sorry, dearest,' he said, 'but I've got appointments at eleven and twelve.'

She wore a little severe smile. 'I suppose it doesn't matter that it's my last day!'

'Of course it matters!' How unfair of her to put it like that! But he spoke gently, to propitiate her, knowing in advance with a kind of horror that she was not to be propitiated, for he had offended deeply in some way. 'We're not losing so very much time, are we?' he asked. 'We're together, after all. It isn't so important where we happen to be.'

'We're not together,' she said. 'We've been separated.'

He didn't quite understand. 'I made my engagements,' he said, 'before I knew you were coming.'

And he would keep them: he said it suddenly to himself with an access of heat. It was most reasonable to keep engagements. Moreover, the obscure will in him was set on resisting her.

'I simply don't understand you, Adrian.' Her voice was extremely cold. 'You put your work first, I suppose, and me second.'

'Really, I don't understand you, either.' It was horrifying to hear sarcasm in her tone, to see scorn in her eyes. Was this Linet, that had been so loving yesterday? Linet or no, contempt was not acceptable to his pride. 'It's nonsense to say that,' he began, with temper rising. 'Why are you so cross with me? What have I said or done, after all?'

'Do have a little imagination,' she replied. 'You're dealing with a woman, not with the subject of a window.'

'I know.' He still tried to get a grip of himself, though it seemed as if she were not listening. This was not Linet. 'All I want is to make you happy.'

'Then why not do what's obvious? I came all the way over here to see you. . . .'

'That's unfair.' If she was not to be conciliated, he would be a bit sharp. 'You came because you wanted to, I suppose?'

'Quite. Have a little manners, and let me finish what I was going to say.'

'Very well.' Adrian had the sensation that a barrage had come down. Then let her say what she had to, even if it was fatal; for he would not tolerate contempt, even for love. All at once he felt the hot rush of anger to his brain. 'You used to tell me I knew how to deal with a woman,' he added, still trying to control his voice. But he could hear what was harsh and ugly in it.

'Let's talk of me, not of a woman.'

'By all means.' An age-old savage resumed charge of Adrian. 'By all means. I've no wish to generalize . . . If we must talk this nonsense. . . .'

'Oh!' It was a cry. She got down from the window-seat. 'You knew how to get me, certainly. But you evidently don't know how to keep me.'

Why should one bother to keep this little termagant! He had been about to say it. But she was going, this effigy of Linet, and fury died out in a cold flow of dismay. It was preposterous that this should be taking place. He seemed to see clearly, without understanding it, that he had lost Linet, lost her some time this morning. What word of his, what look, had extinguished the light in her; what harsh breath had blown out her spirit? It was not Linet who dealt with him, but some imperious, hard girl: Linet herself, innocent, fairy-bred, dearly loved, was wandering bodiless, homeless, unconjurable, in the universe. And Adrian was destroyed by his own rage: there could never re-exist the man who had been guiltless towards her.

It was for him to speak. 'Are you going?' Impossible, surely, that they should part without some little warm recollection.

'I wouldn't stay one moment for any other man,' Linet said. 'Have you something to say?'

Pride still resented her tone; but his grief was the greater. 'Perhaps it was not we who were arguing, but other selves in us, natures that can't stand the tension of love, and revolt against what our spirit demands.'

'It's late to be philosophical,' she replied.

'You know well,' he argued, 'that love like ours is beyond what is natural. You yourself didn't believe it possible to last . . .'

'It looks rather as if I'm right.'

'Don't be so cold, Linet!' His nerves uttered a cry. He put an arm round her and kissed her.

She was indifferent. 'You drove me away. I can't come back just when you whistle for me.'

Again a flare-up of his abominable pride. Why, after all, should he bother? Let her get over it by herself. He had been about to say so; but despair for this foolish disaster suddenly forbade him. Perhaps the misery in his face a little appeased her, for she conceded: 'There may be something to be said between us. I'll discuss it. You see Adrian. . . .'

But all life and desire had left him, and in his turn he made the refusal. 'I have a horror of discussion and explanations,' he said, he who had himself just tried to begin one. She was pulling on her gloves. She wore a smile. 'Explanations don't make things right,' he explained: 'they come right in another way, in a mysterious way, without a word said. A miracle takes place. . . .'

'There are no miracles,' said Linet. 'You cannot bring back the dead.' She left the tower.

136

3

IT was towards evening, in July. Bella, Mark and
Adrian sat in the drawing-room, waiting for visitors.
Bella sewed, Mark grinned over a volume of car-
toons, Adrian contemplated the sage in the wall-
landscape, a bald old gentleman with a wisp of
white beard and a great stomach; a ribald, profound man, ugly and celestial, reclining under a
tree with arm affectionately round flagon, wearing
an expression of extreme awareness towards some
voice or influence in a spray of leaves. There was
in that comical rapt face a secret that might cure this
malady of the soul. Adrian, in some hour when he
stood on the threshold of enlightenment, copied
the figure from a silk in the British Museum;
brought the Presence to his own house. He had not
understood it; he only felt that all significance was
grasped in this symbol, and he would see it but for
some hindrance.

At the moment it was difficult to contemplate,
difficult to rid his mind of unpleasant emotions. His
thoughts swayed now one way, now another, like
a crowd organized by passions. That made him
angrier with Linet. Strange, after what passed
between them in France, that it needed an effort
to remember her with tenderness; but she had
injured his spontaneity, distracted him, deprived
his creative energy of its proper joy, and he was

exhausted with going over the situation in his mind. It was his idea, just now, to see what consolation there was in work or in things somewhat more universal than himself, if they could be felt or got at. He decided on a brutal disregard of his own feelings. It was the more irritating, therefore, that whereas there had been moments (he must admit it) when her absence would have brought relief in some way or at any rate simplification, in practice her departure meant nothing but pain which it cost great effort to disregard.

It would have been easier to cope with the anguish of final parting. But that was not the state of affairs; he felt certain they were only parted until some change took place in them both. There had been an exchange of letters, in which Linet, although she apologized for her part in the quarrel (and Adrian promptly replied that he wished to take responsibility), seemed finally to lay the blame on him: this hurt him in the most foolish proud remnant of his unregenerate He. But there was something cold in her letter. He perceived the inhumanity of that fairylike person in a most freezing aspect. He wrote in a kind of pride, to accept the blame, and the act paralysed his love for her; they remained apart. He had no doubt there would be a moment when her own coldness would give way in misery and longing. He was resolved to make no move until somehow his mind ran clear and her image was bright again. 'If there is to be a miracle,' she wrote, mocking, as he supposed, words used at their parting,

'that will be more to do with you than with me.'
Oh, would it? Adrian hardened, even though he
understood in the very moment that these thoughts,
these emotions, this wickedness (whatever might be
the case on her side) proceeded from an Adrian who
should have died when Linet gave up her heart to
him. In any case, this resurrected savage had no
claim to her heart, this creature subject to anger,
vengefulness, jealousy . . . Adrian turned sharply
in his chair. His thoughts all swayed in one direction, for what faith was there, now all she believed about love had come true, what morality
in that unmoral creature, to stop her giving herself
anywhere, in sheer carelessness, in mockery of her
own folly. . .?

This would not do. Adrian strove to set his
thoughts on the Sage, a being who was not distracted,
for whom all things were Now. What was the
nature of that merriment, what laughter shook that
belly? Fat and clean-fleshed as fruit, profound
and baby-innocent, ribald and spiritual, he drank
with his shadow and heard a voice in his big toe.
The secret is beyond me, Adrian reflected. I am
no philosopher, and never shall be. I am a disconnected artist living from day to day by some
remote truth just catched out of the press of things.
I only know truth when I produce it; I only speak
truth under the form of art. My fate is to entangle
myself with the beauty and sadness of manifested
things. This Sage contemplates the infinite, that
contains all forms. He does not grieve over imper-

manence. He will not weep for a lost love, but accept another. He has no need to save himself from passion or express himself in creating.

The front-door bell rang on the other side of the wall, destroying the illusion of far-stretching landscape, mountain, forest and waterfall. The occupants of the room stirred. 'It is strange,' was Adrian's last thought, 'that I can scarcely recall Linet.'

Bella came and tucked in the loop under his collar. 'Cheer up,' she said. 'You look miserable.' She scanned his face. 'You don't seem well. You need a change.'

'So do you,' he said. 'I'll take you to Switzerland.' Mrs. Mansfield came in with Marigold, Viola and Frances, followed by Mr. Mansfield and Andrew. Adrian enjoyed acting as host; he was able to put his misery a little way back, for the time being. Sherry was offered on the terrace, in evening sunshine. 'The holly trees look sombre at this time of year,' he said. 'A little dusty and vanquished, as if Christmas has been put in a museum. Christmas will come again, I suppose.' He shuddered. 'The sun will be withdrawn, and our life die once more.'

'You should come to Buenos Aires with us.' Frances said. 'Couldn't you?'

'It's very kind of you . . .' Everybody who desired sherry was served; everyone was in conversation.

'Well, how are things?' Mr. Mansfield enquired. Adrian gave information, though Mr. Mansfield

140

always seemed to divine how things were without it. 'Very good,' Adrian said, 'since that private view of Pollock's library. A man offered me a church in Germany, and another windows for a house in Park Lane. Other things have come along too. In particular an entomologist, a friend of Pollock's, is making a laboratory, an insectarium, or whatever it is. I am to do him some windows.' His mind, while it had lost enthusiasm, was not giving attention to this project; but he remembered and finished it up from where he had cast it, to be worked on, perhaps unnoticed.

Adrian found a little taste of forgetfulness, of enjoyment, in the summer dining-room, the flowers, the old clock on the mantelpiece blinded by a stroke of the sun, the glass creatures and water-plants in a bowl on the table, light in a decanter and in the windows. What a beautiful colour, the sherry! A pleasure paid for with some project of his own mind, executed with the assistance of Mark and others. Adrian glanced at Mark, who had no sadness; no desire and no sadness; no life, one might say, and no death. Bella too. Had there been desire in Bella, until pain or some morality from the grim north chastened it? Ah, well. Vigorous and creative natures receive more grievous lessons . . . It was necessary to dish out the langouste. Adrian gave himself to the pleasure of food and wine, remembering the sage and his flagon.

'No,' Mark answered to Marigold, 'I don't seem to care much about holidays. There have been some nice trips to Asia Minor; but that was to do a job. I'm amused all the time, if you know what I mean, by the things I do.' He grinned with a kind of frightening shyness over this bit of self-revelation.

'What are you doing this year,' asked Adrian.

'Nothing much,' Mrs. Mansfield said, 'because of our long trip to Buenos Aires in the winter. We have taken a house on the Thames from now till October.'

'Do come some of the time,' urged Frances. 'We can have some fishing.'

Mrs. Mansfield confirmed the invitation. 'If you're not tired of us. A week-end, at least.'

'A week-end, certainly. Thank you.' It was tactful of the Mansfields, Adrian thought, not to have asked him too definitely: one should not make a habit of people, or of oneself. Linet had thought that all along. He wondered by what instinct the girls avoided the name of Linet. He noted that for the moment he had no need of her company. It was curious how the meaning of Linet died in his mind. He drank hock, and prepared to carve a couple of fine plump ducks. He carved expertly, and with affection.

'You relish food?' Mr. Mansfield watched with his miss-nothing eyes.

'I relish all pleasure,' Adrian replied. 'I could make it my profession. And sometimes I see the beauty of asceticism and pursue it for weeks at a time.' He grinned, remembering the Sage's belly, his clean flesh, his intent face. 'What a strange smile,' young Frances said.

There seemed suddenly to be an opinion in the room that Adrian was a strange man. He became grave, and experienced fear of something hellish in himself that might destroy him. He drank claret with the duck, and longed to amend all equivocation in his nature, lighten all darkness in himself. He determined on it, with all the force of his will.

He sat a good while over port with Mr. Mansfield, Andrew, and Mark. Andrew was simple, certainly; one would say there was no distortion in him. Adrian envied that simple affection between father and son, that honesty of attitude. He would like to be a man of fifty or so with a grown-up son who treated him as a friend. Possibly — Adrian mused over his glass and watched evening lights gleaming in the table furniture — possibly there was no such thing as simplicity in men, no honesty between father and son. He found it difficult to understand, knowing himself and remembering his own father.

Mr. Mansfield spoke to him as it were confidentially when they were half-way to the drawing-room. 'Linet's case will come on in the autumn.'

'Oh. So soon?'

'She should be free, therefore, next summer.'

'Good,' said Adrian.

'She writes to us that her Belgians settle in Antwerp shortly — in September, I think. You knew, of course.'

'Yes, I knew. She seems to be happy with them.' Adrian used a light voice; but he knew that Mr.

Mansfield was already aware of estrangement. It annoyed him.

'Her happiness depends on you,' Mr. Mansfield said. 'You are the only person in the world who can give her happiness.'

'Surely not! Linet is independent. She is a light to herself, I should have said, as people should be. She's not a girl who would ever depend on a man for her happiness.'

Mr. Mansfield looked at him with amusement.

'It's a responsibility,' Adrian said.

'Of course it is. But it's yours.' Mr. Mansfield robustly put forward the fact. Adrian protested within himself. Good Lord, it was enough to have the responsibility of one's talent, without the addition of a woman's happiness! 'We'd better go to the drawing-room, don't you think?' He showed the way, still fuming, oppressed by the complexity and weight of things.

Bella was entertaining with self-possession and no fuss. Bella regarded character. She had reduced it to a few essentials; if people exhibited these she did not inspect the outward parts of their personalities, and she was not impressed by wealth, station, or any circumstance. Adrian almost resented her self-containment. He suggested dancing. Mark, a wretched but enthusiastic performer, took Marigold, Adrian took Mrs. Mansfield and Mr. Mansfield took his young daughter Frances. Viola sat with Bella. Then Adrian took Frances, and then Marigold. Last of all he took Viola, surprised to find that his heart ran a little fast. It was a kind of embarrassment, because of what passed between them in France; unnecessary, for she had shown no sign all evening. She remained tranquil now. It might just as well have been Marigold that he danced with. Rather a pity! Adrian suddenly smiled, remarking his own honesty. He met an answering grin in the eyes of that Sage as they twirled by. Yes, it would have given taste to the evening if she had shown remembrance. Her conduct was prescribed, perhaps; she must know he was supposed to be going to marry Linet, and Linet was a great friend. But passion is ruthless and without morality. How would Viola conduct herself if he tempted her? For himself, by some unexamined law in his mind, he refrained from anything that might have led her to make acknowledgment: a strange thing. He reflected on it a long time when they had gone, sitting face to face with the sage, raising a whisky and soda in answer to his flagon. For the Sage seemed to advise acquiescence in the order of events. Take what comes, he seemed to say, without longing for what cannot be recovered. Take Viola. One thing doesn't spoil another, and doesn't replace it. Many things exist at once. People who want the whole of a thing must lose it. The sage did appear to say something of this kind; but when one looked in his face it wore a most baffling expression.

4

ADRIAN was powerfully creative. In the heat of
August, among sultry trees and scents and in deep-
ening light, his tense mood began to resolve itself
in rich thoughts and visions. While he tended great
veined poisonous plants in the greenhouse the
thoughts opened in his mind with an effect of surprise and conviction. He had thought it impossible
that he should ever go inside that greenhouse again,
where he and Linet had vision together — vision,
or experience, of something more than the substance
of art; but considerations of sentiment gave way
when he found, on going there in an impulsive,
despairing minute to recover some feeling of her
existence, that the air of the place and presence of
strange growths favoured creation. It was at least
satisfactory that his powers should flourish. Yes,
it was an achievement that when a few moments'
relaxation of the will might bring on a crisis of
regret, of longing, of jealousy, of anger, the powers
that owned him should abolish that lesser person
and dominate. And there was a sense — he acknowledged this with a side-glance — in which he dreaded
the arrival of any letter of love or appeal from Linet
as a demand on his attention.

But in September he felt the need of release from
the scene of so much conflict and wrote to the
Mansfields. They replied, inviting him for a few

146

days; inviting Bella as well, and Mark, if he cared. Mark did not care, and Bella refused, out of what seemed to Adrian an irrational obstinacy; she preferred her own house, she said; she didn't like travelling; people thought too much about holidays. Adrian went therefore by himself, rather wondering what made him go where he was so likely to be reminded of Linet.

In everything the Mansfields recognized and took what was fine; they enjoyed an amplitude of convenience. They were at present in an old house among trees, with lawns and gardens. At the river's edge a fine stone wall with vases of geraniums and a sweep of steps either end enclosed a lily-thick, fish-peopled harbour. There were boats and punts under a shed up a green backwater. It was sweet air to sleep in after the sultry nights in St. John's Wood, and Adrian, before he drifted into oblivion on a tide of scents from the fields, had to harden his pride against an absent companion. It was becoming quite easy for him to employ his will in this way. 'It is better than anything,' he said, 'to be alone. There is no life of the spirit without prolonged solitude, especially the solitude of deep night. I no longer fear solitude.' It was gratifying to note that. Through the experiences of the past year or two in art and in love he had attained a measure of self-establishment. It was queer to know for oneself the truth of old sayings, and find out in experience that the result of his attempt to put himself at the disposal of powers resident in what is other than the personal was a sense of increased stability in the universe, greater efficacy in art and in love. Yet he turned restlessly, aware of some danger in this attitude of mind.

Adrian altogether abandoned work for the time being, and tried to relax. It was pleasant, though he was restless, to spend these days with the Mansfields, swimming in the reach that swept round to Benson lock on the one hand and Shillingford on the other, fishing for gudgeon or perch and hoping for pike by the reeds beyond Shillingford bridge, pursuing excursions up the winding green tunnels of the Thames, or, if they were tired of the river, playing tennis on that lawn before the house. Sometimes Adrian would draw. They were such graceful, frank children; and it was always delightful that one might meet Viola, or Marigold, or Frances on the stairs or in some passage or room, or else take one of them fishing. They and the quiet country somehow made it seem natural that he should accept calmly an unnatural state of affairs and forget to revolve it.

On the fifth afternoon he took the fishing punt and went with Viola to a backwater not far from the house. He would draw while she fished; or he would fish himself. It was a hot, lazy afternoon. They seemed shut away from the world in that tangle of trees and bushes and cow-parsley, except that there was Marigold already reading in the fork of a willow, and there through a gap in the tangle were several of the children and their friends,

148

streaming along the edge of a wheat-field. Adrian decided to fish. He and Viola put out their rods. They knew there were fat roach in the pool down there among the reed stalks. The air trembled over the cornfield, the cornstalks stood up motionless, insects flicked the surface of the water, silence fell.

The fish were not anxious to be caught that afternoon. Adrian reflected on the practice of that Chinese gentleman who would not use bait or hook, saying that any fish that desired to be caught would attach itself to his line of its own will. He stared into the water, wondering how they lived down there, what experiences were obtainable if any philosopher should assume the shape of fish or beetle or newt. He was aware that Viola guarded his peace, for when Marigold called to them from her tree Viola enjoined silence with a gesture. Marigold, less respectful of his contemplations, made a face — he saw it with the tail of his eye. He smiled, and allowed himself to become deeply absorbed. The mind, concentrated on the float, took a start sideways, with the submerged half of it, into another world. One got within measure of understanding things. A little more and the secret would be achieved. What secret? The secret of these forms of insect or fish or white lily with broad leaves; what the sage, listened for, what he had. Perhaps there was no secret, nothing to grasp with the mind and display with the power of art. But these Chinese had understood and displayed it: the thing that

149

one perceived in objects of nature was in their pictures, difficult to describe but present. What thing? Adrian had a strong sense of it; but it evaded his comprehension. 'Quick: your float!' There was a cry from Viola; she could not resist her feelings when his float indicated a bite. He transferred attention to the slim quill, and the world he explored was abolished. The rod bent: 'At least it isn't a dead branch or an old kettle,' said Adrian. It was a strong fish that had to be drawn away from the shadows under the tangle of trees, away from the water-lilies in front of the reeds. Adrian added it presently to the population of roach, perch, gudgeon, eels and young pike that inhabited the tank. 'It's a pity to use bait,' he said, putting fresh paste on the hook, 'but I haven't the strength of mind not to.'

'A strange thing to say?' Viola invited an explanation, watching him with deep eyes. She looked so pretty in her white frock and shady hat; her cheek was so soft and brown; her look so deep; she was pure and cool and slight like the lily. What was behind her calm and friendly demeanour? He gave a quick thought to it and smiled at her, and went back to the world of insects and water-plants.

They became so still that a kingfisher stood long enough on a twig for Adrian to study him; and when Viola too had a bite and she lifted her rod and the bird flashed out of sight Adrian drew him. Viola bent over to look at the confection of lines and touches. 'Oh!' she exclaimed, 'it's a kingfisher! I've watched them so often!'

Adrian smiled over his success in representation — if that was the word. 'Why do you sometimes smile at me?' she asked. 'I smile at myself,' he answered, escaping at once from the danger of entanglement in personal relations, seizing an opportunity, or accepting an obligation, to discriminate his specific quality as artist in relation to the body of human achievement in that field, and understand the nature of his particular talent in order to obey it. This was more than representation, he perceived. You are old-fashioned, he told himself, and extremely peculiar. You have become the vessel of a most ancient tradition; the exponent, rather, of an antique spirit. With a modern, a highly individual technique, assuredly. What is your idea? he enquired. To apprehend the last rhythms, to display the real form of things by the means of art, to construct a vehicle for the communication of whatever indescribable substance, or being, is back of the seen world. An impudent ambition! And just how was this to be done? By emptying the mind, becoming nothing. When you are nothing you will be all other things; the work of your hand will manifest the essence of transitory things. . . .

Adrian sat with head bent and hands clasped on his rod, unconscious of it, filled with vision, in a manner of speaking at prayer. He was empty now; empty of his own being, intensely aware of the being in cornfield, water-plant and dragon-fly that hummed from point to point in the dense growth about the pool. He was in conversation with a ladybird, brilliant red speck on the green blade of a reed. He had the experience of the ladybird and the reed. But there was something more, something in the ladybird and the reed not subject to death; and it would be given if he made no effort. Yes, he was much cleansed in body and mind. Something was about to be communicated. He made a little gesture, as if to grasp meaning; but meaning eluded him, and in place of what had been the substance of his experience just now there came to his waking senses and cleansed heart the picture of Linet. He stood up, rocking the punt, and stretched out his hand for her.

[- 5 -]

ADRIAN believed in miracles, as between Linet and himself. There had been a miracle, and he contemplated the shining fact forgetful of all else, the recent past, worldly circumstances, details of her whereabouts, practicability and all that. He knew where to find her. She would be in the Cathedral in Antwerp, at Benediction, on Sunday. He was so sure that he allowed himself to doubt it, steaming up the Schelde in a glory of daybreak. That dismal interregnum was obliterated; there was no past since the last minute of their felicity. The steamer zigzagged up the river, between sandbanks. Beautiful flat country, Belgium on the one side, green, lucid; Holland on the other, woods and church towers, roofs of small towns in the distance. To-morrow, perhaps, he would go somewhere like that with Linet, in a little train. They would sit close together, and he would twine his fingers with hers; or if they were alone in the carriage he would take her on his knee. All country was a garden where they were together. Those months had been all nightmare. He had no life without her; she was his air, the condition of his existence. He rocked to and fro remembering what had been between them in fear she might forget or reject it. But if there is one sure piece of knowledge, he said to the golden east, it is that things are with Linet as they are with

153

me; this change will have taken place in her soul as well.

Of course, there were many reasons why she might not appear in the Cathedral. He walked up and down the deck, considering chances, gazing now at the little waves that curled outwards from the bows, now at the foam thrashed up by the propellers, white dawnlike stuff, tossing, falling, shining in this brilliance of early morning! She might be away. She might have some engagement. Well, then, he would go every day and wait in the Cathedral until she came. Adrian snuffed the keen air and felt his unshaven chin. There would be plenty of time for shaving; all morning and half afternoon. He had not bothered to hire a cabin, wishing rather to sit up all night and look over the rail into that blackness of the sea, that space and nothingness to which came the radiant image of Linet, riding beside the ship. He did not know where she lived — letters had been sent, while she was travelling, to an arranged address. But she had settled in Antwerp with her Belgians; and Adrian remembered that Sunday was her birthday. She would certainly be in the Cathedral, Linet who belonged to no church and lived by a light seen in heaven.

Presently the roofs and towers of Antwerp could be seen, and the Cathedral, that shape within which the miracle of their reunion would take place this afternoon: no doubt of it. Adrian wondered about his own feeling for churches, especially dark and

Gothic ones with solemn windows. I haven't really
got any sense of God, he said, although I seem to
feel the Presence in churches: no doubt that is
something else. I wish I had a sense of God's being.
But my parents murdered it. Can such a thing be
restored? How life would change, how everything
would fall in its place, how without fear or passion
I should be, if I had that sense! But at the moment
these reflections were without force, for he was in
great vigour of early morning and hungry. He
went downstairs for some coffee, and filled his heart
with the thought of Linet.

The steamer tied up, the passengers disembarked.
Adrian drove to the big hotel near the station where
he had stayed with Linet. The familiarity of the
place — the long garish foyer with its grilles and
counters where they had come so happily to engage
their room, the dining-room like that of a liner, and
more especially the rooms where they had lived and
slept — affected him so that he had to keep back
tears. The same high room with the great window
looking over the square, and the two beds; the
same luxurious bathroom where Linet could lie
at full length in a sort of porcelain sarcophagus; the
same florid ante-room, with its crimson curtains
and mantelpiece a little faded, gilded mirrors a
little tarnished, tapestried sofas and armchairs a little
worn, round table with patterned tablecloth a
little ink-stained, rich carpet a little trodden away.
They had liked this slightly tarnished splendour.
They had littered their books and newspapers on

155

the table, thrown their clothes on the sofas, put flowers in the vases, made a delightful piggery of this dimmed magnificence. Adrian did what he could with the contents of his own suit-case to make the room look as much as possible like what they had been used to, as if this might be a means of conjuring Linet back. He went into the bedroom. To-night her stockings would be lying folded on a neat pile of clothes, on that chair. His heart stopped when he suddenly thought it might not be so.

For all he could do in the way of self-control, Adrian found it impossible not to lunch early, and he was in the Cathedral long before there was any chance of her being there. He sat where he could study the pictures, or contemplate the high altar. What a clean, light and sensible church! The priests were different from what one saw in Latin countries — shaved, energetic, theological men, more interested in conduct, one would say, than in ritual. The Presence was that of a venerable and imposing burgomaster. The place was Dutch in some way. Linet would fit in, entering in her clean skirt and neat jacket of yellow linen. She would be wearing that. He arrived at an insight of many things in Dutch and Flemish art, particularly a certain experience of light . . . yes, her face was very clear in his mind's eye, vivid as ever, and sad. At this moment he understood fully why she had been sad in Paris, those weeks when they were waiting to become lovers: it was the time of annunciation for her. There were several elements in her sadness, such as regret for her marriage, out of which she must have hoped much; reluctance to enter once again with all the force of her nature, as she was bound to do even against the advice of her intelligence, in relations with a man, and exchange all possibilities for one improbable adventure. But more than all was the terrible knowledge that she was fatally in love, that love was her genius and destiny, that she was singled out as a victim for this exaltation and grief. It was not until she had been able to accept this that she sent for him. How saint-like and dedicated she had been than afternoon in the Luxembourg Gardens! He saw clearly now, and turned his face to the altar, making vows. For it was her conviction that Adrian was destined for some other love, in earth or heaven. He vowed to remove that sadness. If you could see my thoughts and feelings, he said to her likeness, you would know that you are my life for ever, the realization of all I ever wished for, a perfect and everlasting fact, out of which, can you not see, this miracle has come? For me there is no other possibility in a woman. If I come to the end of you, I must look for God. Whom I do not yet know.

He became aware that somewhere outside, beyond the roof like angel's music, a carillon was ringing; and at the same moment that Linet was advancing down the main aisle, small in that great space and demure, like a little girl. She looked round with an eager expression, and he knew that she had looked round in that way many times, for him. Her

157

face was intent and sad; and Adrian, when he observed her sadness, tasted the bitterness of human existence. But Linet came to his side with a twist; and it became clear from her eyes that the miracle had been fully accomplished between them.

[- 6 -]

'You wouldn't expect a woman not to weep a little!' Linet dabbed her eyes with a handkerchief produced from a surprising part of her attire.

'You make such big tears. They spurt into your tea,' Adrian said.

They were having tea side by side on a red sofa in a café in the Avenue de Keyser. At the counter, opposite, a girl was serving customers with cream cakes. 'She is exactly like an old portrait of a Queen of France,' said Adrian. 'I call her remarkably interesting.'

'So do I,' said Linet. 'If I were you I'd rather have her than me. I should know how to deal with her.'

'You're beginning to be yourself,' Adrian replied.

'I suppose you've been making love to Viola,' Linet suggested.

Adrian was angry. 'Why do you say a thing like that!'

'Well, haven't you?'

'I don't want to make love to Viola. I'm not in love with her. If I were I should tell you.'

'I hope so.' Linet said it gravely.

But at present there was no possiblity of misunderstanding between them, and to be angry was a satisfying piece of lover's impudence. In fact, their talk was irrelevant: they were occupied with

159

some profounder conversation, telling one another what there was no mistaking. No stopping, either. Linet recognized this. Adrian, in a sober moment, appreciated a number of facts in the situation; Linet appreciated them, too, but she made no account of them. 'I love you,' he said, 'in that yellow linen and that mushroom hat and those neat shoes. It makes you so little-girl. You're also like a September leaf. But I am a lunatic.'

'Why?'

'I was thinking you might have joined me in the hotel.'

'Well, I shall. Naturally.'

'But you've got a job here.'

'It would be wicked if we didn't spend the night together. Several nights.'

'That's right, according to heaven. I only thought of the risk on earth. Perhaps we ought to go somewhere else?'

'No. We must be where we were before. Don't you understand that?'

'So well that I've got our place ready.'

When he told her that he had taken their familiar suite and put flowers in it and tried to give it some air of her presence her tears spilled over again. 'Well,' she said, 'if you see things like that, as I do, isn't it inevitable?'

'It's what I hoped for,' he answered. 'But I wondered if you could get away from your Belgian brat.'

'I shall simply ask for a holiday. As a matter of

160

fact they're very nice people; and they asked if I'd like to go home for my birthday. I said no. Now I shall say yes. And if they don't like it they can get on with it.'

'You're a decided young person,' Adrian said.

'I am. I've always just let people get on with it, especially men, if they didn't like what I said or did. I never expected to alter myself for anybody; but I shall try, for you.'

'I don't want you to alter yourself,' he replied. 'I want the authentic Linet, imperious, intractable, intolerant, satirical, and all the other things she is.'

'Am I like that?' Linet looked checked for a minute. 'There are things I'll talk to you about in a few days. I'll telephone now, and then you must take me in a taxi to get my things.'

'We could get everything new, if you like,' Adrian suggested.

'You can do that when you marry me. I'm still . . .' She corrected herself. 'No you shall do what you like. But I'd rather have my own things.'

'Come on then.' In a few minutes they were driving side by side in a taxi, and Adrian gave himself up to the fact that they were together, and in love, and free as angels.

[- 7 -]

'IT is given to you and me while in this world to enjoy the felicity of some region where it is less troublesome to be oneself.'

'I achieve existence in you,' she said. 'How dark and You you looked when you said that. It was marvellous to wake up and see those intent eyes looking at me.' She shrank under the bedclothes and looked out at him like some bright animal. 'Oh dear! I feel safe. I won't ever leave this room or this bed.'

The coffee-tray was on a little table between them. A golden September morning filled the window. Beyond, out of sight down there behind the high window-sill, was the world, no concern of theirs.

'There are times when I really don't know if I'm in this world or some other,' Adrian went on. 'For example, last night, when we walked in those silent dark streets and squares with cobblestones, and heard the carillon somewhere in the air above us; or when it came true that we were actually here together, and you were there soaping yourself in the bath. It seemed too much happiness.'

'I'm too much unhappy,' Linet said. 'It's partly through being a woman. But you can't know what it feels like. I don't know what takes hold of me

162

sometimes, like when we quarrel. Hell ! Who'd be a woman?'

'I'm glad you were made one.'

'You're the only fact that reconciles me to it, Adrian. Men have a much better time of it. They have affairs much more in their own hands. They're not so absolutely in the power of their physical condition, and not so dependent for their happiness on some initiative outside themselves. If I were a man, Adrian, I'd take a lot of initiative; and I'd never allow myself to be tied up with anybody. So I shall be bound to agree with you if you suddenly leave me.'

'You wouldn't think like that if you really were a man,' Adrian said. 'Men have a good deal of heart, you know.'

'They shouldn't have. Women aren't worth it.' She got out of bed in her earnestness and began vigorously brushing her hair, counting a hundred. Adrian watched her and the movement of her arms, extremely contented with the graceful apparition in half-buttoned pyjamas. Wasn't it satisfying enough to possess such grace, to be such a pretty piece? Perhaps not, owing to intelligence. But it was enough to be Linet, if she only knew. 'And that reminds me,' Linet went on. 'You've to go back to your work the minute you want to, without considering me. I want you always to put it first.'

Adrian protested that he didn't want to. 'We don't want to talk about it, either,' he said. But

163

she went on with this conversation from the bath, while he shaved in front of the wardrobe mirror in their bedroom, with a view of her through the door. 'It really comes first,' she said. 'It ought to. I've accepted that, and I really do see it. I think it's very important, much more important than a mere person. Why do you smile?' She stopped a moment to regard him. 'It was only when I accepted it that I could unfreeze again,' she went on.

'But I don't want my work to come first! Damn it! I'm in love with you.'

She smiled over the side of the bath. 'Yes, I know. You'll take me when you want me. But I shall only be your mistress. Your own soul is your wife.'

Adrian was perplexed in his feelings, and did not know what to answer. He didn't want to go on with the conversation, anyway. It seemed wrong, some-how, in its terms.

'I shall always be there when you want me,' she said; and he had some inkling of the struggle there must have been before she could come to that conclusion.

'I wrote you horrible letters,' she continued, playing with the sponge. 'I'm afraid I'm difficult.'

'By God!' he burst out. 'The more difficult the better! You're a man's job, Linet, and I like it!' He wiped his face clean and went and kissed her in the bath, soapy and all.

They took train in the afternoon for Blanken-berghe, and enjoyed the dismal vulgarity of that

164

place from the safety of their own passionate contentment. 'I shall always be ready to suffer,' she said, 'if any day like to-day when you take pleasure in me gives your work illumination.'

'You look at this matter with one eye,' he replied. 'The truth is that you are the absolute condition of my work. You're a fact of greater importance than the weather. Now I must have Linet as well as air, food and drink.'

She smiled to herself — ironically, he thought. But now she agreed to put this subject away, and they began to live, with their peculiar capacity for shared experience, one satisfying life. They saw things with one enjoyment and had the same thought at once. 'It's marvellous to be both one and separate,' Adrian said, 'so that we can know each other and the anguish and pleasure of wanting.'

'As long as we're at one really. There's another kind of separation that's simply death.'

'I mean as things are between us now. It's important, I think, in love, for one to withhold himself from the other for continued want in seeking and surprise in giving and taking. Love requires a difficult selfishness. More than anything a lover must preserve his integrity; and refrain from encroachment.'

'You talk in language that I'm only just getting used to,' she said, 'and I don't think I agree with what you say. But it doesn't matter. I've been wondering whether we ought not always to see each other in strange places.'

'I wonder, too. It helps; but we have to achieve independence of circumstances before we can call ourselves accomplished in graceful methods of living.'

'You think we've a long way to go?'

'Certainly, my cat: with the responsibility of a tremendous beginning.'

'I'm glad. But it's frightening.'

They seemed gifted to obtain the taste of their experience without losing it. This happened at odd moments, when they were walking about the streets, visiting some church, or strolling across the square from the Paon Royal, where they usually took their meals; as well as at times when they deliberately assayed together some new flavour of things. Their last afternoon they spent in the sombre Antwerp Zoo. 'This place seems to me foreign and fantastical,' Adrian said. 'They mix up giraffes with tigers. I don't know whether the animals are on show or the shrubberies. It gives me ideas.'

'It would!' Linet said. 'It's queer, I quite agree. But their tigers are beautiful ones.'

They walked in dusty paths by dark shrubberies and gloomy ponds. Presently they found a seat. Adrian looked round and sighed. 'It has a beautiful strange melancholy.'

'It's our last afternoon,' Linet replied. 'I don't like melancholy the way you do, my dark one, but I do feel a certain sad peace.'

'I'm not dark,' he protested. 'I'm clear as sunlight.'

166

'Hazy and shimmering as late afternoon light, perhaps, with sadness in it and strange far away things and the end and disappearance of pleasure. All that is in your eyes. Oh dear. It's our last afternoon, if you must go to-night.'

'Yes, I must.' He looked closely at her, but she didn't seem to resent his going. 'I shall come back before very long.'

'Do you still insist that you'll marry me?'

'Yes,' he answered with earnestness. 'Why do you ask?'

'I don't know. I felt sad. I wanted to hear you say yes. I thought that if you didn't I should die.'

Adrian drew her close. There were shadowy thoughts in his mind, and he was training himself to detain and examine shadowy thoughts. What a change there had been in her, that she desired marriage! And — it was queer! — there had been hesitation before he answered yes to her question, hesitation abolished by the earnestness of his answer. A hesitation not to be explained. For he desired nothing else but to spend life with her, with this beautiful, fairy-bred, loving girl. He hugged her suddenly very tight. 'I love you, you sweet spindly creature.'

'I'm not spindly.'

'You are. And we'll have fairy-like spindly children, little fair girls with big unearthly eyes and long legs and hair blowing about their heads like gossamer.'

'Yes? There'll be one called Selena.' She looked

up to him from the crook of his arm like a child that wants to hear more; and he began to make pictures of their children.

'I want them,' she said, with passionate voice. He felt with surprise the intensity of her longing for them, and once again she became new to him.

[- 8 -]

WHEN Adrian put his suit-case on the table, in the middle of their sitting-room, it was impossible to lay destroying hands on that house of their love, where a pair of shoes under a chair, a vase of flowers on bureau or gorgeous mantelpiece, a frock hanging on the door, a newspaper dropped in the fender, seemed to exist as part of some living entity, of which they too were parcel. Linet, with obedient sad face, was helping to pack—he would rather she didn't, but it seemed to gratify her. 'Stop a minute,' he said. 'I have a feeling that if we put in another shirt, we should do wrong.'

'What do you mean?' She stared, without hoping for anything.

'I can't go. I simply can't.'

She turned an elegant cartwheel. 'You mean it?'

'Absolutely.'

Linet had unusual ways of expressing pleasure. She made her whole body dance and quiver, from shoulders to ankles, like a savage in a forest festival. 'Here, stop it!' he said, and seized her. She still quivered and kicked in his arms, like a landed fish, and suddenly sat on the floor to prevent his smacking her, and discussed the situation from there.

They dined, and walked about the streets of the city one more time, and heard the carillon in the darkness above them. It did not feel like the known world, and Linet was fey. That was indeed their suite, rich and grand by the shaded lights, and littered with their familiar things; and that was actually Linet, brushing her teeth, or dangerously showing him a short arm balance on two chairs, or when the lights were out flitting about the room, an ivory figure with dressing-gown floating like wings; but it seemed to Adrian that he was dealing that night with a person from some enchanted country, or that he lay in an enchanted region, or that he was enchanted himself. The forms of things were dim in the great room; the white shape of that witch was beside him on the sofa; he felt the movement of her arms as if he were a harp that she played upon, and knew the mysterious kiss of her mouth on his flesh; her voice, far away, ghostly, was yet Linet's. Her mouth was at his ear, whispering: 'You were dreaming marble. I lay beside some overthrown image, still thinking its hero-thoughts, god-thoughts. Now you wake and put round me terrible gleaming arms.' He lifted and held her up before the stars in the high window, and her voice died.

9

DURING the winter, at dinner, at the house of a man for whom he was doing some work, Adrian met an accountant, a long pale man with a big nose who liked chess. Having in mind a cold letter from the bank, Adrian invited the man to call on him, and engaged him professionally. His name was Gwatkin, and he made a good friend for Mark, who worked out chess problems in trains and omnibuses with portable apparatus, and played with chess-brothers in distant countries by means of postcards.

Adrian was at a period of intense activity and took the matters that the bank brought to notice in his stride. Indeed, he understood things of this kind very well; but in the good old small days it had not seemed worth while to bother a great deal about scientific accounting, and on many occasions when orders were short he and Mark had made up the wages of their retainers out of the small incomes that (with Bella) they inherited from the private fortunes of their parents. But now things were beginning to move on a large scale, and it was necessary to use exact methods of accounting. 'It's only a question of facing the facts,' he observed to Gwatkin, 'in this as in other regions of experience; and here the facts are easy to ascertain.' And how much more satis-factory, he reflected, to swallow the truth; after the purgative, what ease of mind! Henceforth, much book-keeping, analysis, verification; continuous attention to costs.

The structure of his enterprise was simple, of course; and Gwatkin soon had command of it. 'If I may say so,' he remarked, 'your private expenditure is erratic.'

'I know.' Adrian grinned. 'My plan is to spend money so that it becomes necessary to make it. I make what there is made, you know. We may as well be clear that if I didn't exist the business wouldn't exist either. It would be right if I paid Mark a salary, gave Bella an allowance, and kept the rest for myself, or put it back in the firm. But in fact I've never spent more than my share, or else I've paid back what I borrowed.'

'And created no reserves; none to speak of,' the accountant said. 'In future you must all three have salaries, and they mustn't be exceeded until the show yields more. No going to the bank and drawing out what you feel like spending.'

'In a year,' said Adrian solemnly, 'our salaries will be immense. The reserves too.' He enjoyed the sensations of invincible energy. There was so much work he could get, so many things he could do, from making simple windows for somebody's vestibule to decorating an entire cathedral. He had his ideas for mosaic work, for altars, candlesticks, all kinds of furniture. There were a lot of people he could go and see . . . one might have to fall in a little with their ideas . . . 'But mind this,' he added: 'I won't undertake a single piece of work that I don't enjoy. I'll grow rich because people come and ask for the work I produce.'

Long Gwatkin smiled the pale smile of one who began life with such hopes.

'My method is correct,' Adrian said. 'Seek first the kingdom of God — that is, produce what is in you to produce, exert and purify your specific talent — and the other things will be added.'

'You're a queer bloke,' said Gwatkin.

So are you, Adrian thought. Adrian was good for Gwatkin, a man overgrown and delicate, intelligent and practical, but without that gift of genius or sheer eupepsia that gives men dominion over their fellows. He had begun to turn his face from the lights that he followed when young. The days of ardent and idiotic discussion were long past; the days of passionate reading were becoming rare; it was often a burden to hear music; he no longer hoped to meet some woman who should justify life and the world. He was in any case a man for whom the after taste of experience was bitter. 'If ever I go with a woman,' he said to Adrian, 'I suffer hell from bad conscience.' He said this to Adrian in the first few days of their acquaintance, and Adrian, looking at his pale face and dusty hair, discovered something about his mouth, perhaps a pursing or some expression of the colourless lips, that was a trifle unpleasant. Gwatkin in fact had soon displayed a taste, almost an itch, for bawdy stories. At the third or fourth Adrian revolted, for what was said seemed to touch Linet and himself, and with indignation he said 'I don't want to hear.' Gwatkin was astonished. So was Adrian, for he understood the man's state of mind by what he remembered of his own, years ago.

'I don't want to sound like a prig,' he said presently, reflecting that he had himself exchanged one or two particularly witty ones with Linet; 'but it touches something important in my experience.'

After that conversation Gwatkin became once more the long thoughtful man with pleasant manners of their first acquaintance. He had a way of listening, a respect for your personality, that Adrian liked. They collaborated. They turned the enterprise into a limited company. Gwatkin came round often in the evenings and played chess with Mark. When Linet comes, Adrian thought, watching him one night, he'll fall in love with her. I wonder if Mark will. Probably not. Mark is fulfilled: Gwatkin isn't. It will be surprising if Mark doesn't, all the same.

Adrian worked prodigiously all winter. He enquired about insects and plants; read about them, and made innumerable drawings. Mark also practised the representation of insects' wings. In his efforts after adequate expression Adrian discovered, for the second time in his career, a new process and a new shade of colour. He took Mark and Gwatkin down to the kiln and chortled over some pieces in the trays, like a witch cooking.

He solved also some special problems regarding irradiation. Yet that was all, so to speak, on the side; his main activity was in the conception and deliverance of forms. At night, he adored the image of Linet; and wrapped himself up in the solitude that so fruitfully nourished him. He frequently revolved doubtfully some ideas of Mr. Pollock's regarding celibacy.

The months passed. One day Gwatkin asked if he couldn't see some of Adrian's work, in place. 'Isn't there some church in the neighbourhood,' he enquired, 'where I could see a few of your saints in their proper gloom?'

Adrian grinned. 'No church. But I could show you some figures in a library.' They went to the Reverend Eugene Pollock's house on a Sunday, about half-past twelve. The clergyman was just come in after morning service, and offered champagne with caviare sandwiches. 'One needs it,' he said. 'But you haven't been to church, I daresay.'

'One needs it all the same,' Adrian replied. 'There's something about Sunday. It affects the digestion, the nerves, the temperament. There's a kind of flatness, as if something vital in the atmosphere went to sleep. It may be just Saturday night, of course. One usually exceeds in some way.'

'In my case a surfeit of preparation,' the clergyman said, 'an excess of discipline. I devote myself to thought, and to prayer.' He looked over his spectacles at Adrian, as if he intended this for a challenge. Then he withdrew the look, as it were, and shook his head as if there were no truth except what a man understood of himself. 'Old clergyman should be put out of the way,' he remarked to the astonished Gwatkin. 'You have not come to see me, I presume, but the windows. What is he, Adrian? A customer?'

'No,' said Adrian, 'an accountant. He's helping me to put things on a sound financial basis.'

'Encouraging news! That will be good for your art. And evidently you intend to relate your ideas to the facts of the world, in the same way.'

'If I understand your meaning, I do. Especially if I can ascertain the facts.' Adrian used a little salt in his voice, answering to what he heard in the Reverend Eugene's. That old gentleman always seemed both friendly and inimical, as if, while he admired the work of Adrian's genius, he felt some dislike of the personal Adrian, or at any rate some duty to warn and chide lest that personal Adrian should stand in the work's way.

They went to the library, and Gwatkin, when the oak doors were thrown open, advanced in an attitude of respect. Curious, thought Adrian, that I, the author of these windows, feel chiefly disappointment. Like God regarding the world, perhaps. Though we cannot think of any incompetence on His part, after all: it is a failure in the material . . . I am no philosopher.

'His windows are altogether less purple than they were,' Mr. Pollock said. 'Purple would not have been suitable for this room, of course. But there is a new brightness and clarity. I even complain of a tendency, here and there, towards a formal geometry. But his figures still live with that intense life of the soul.'

Four windows were now in position in the west wall, and one in the east. The other three in that wall and the large southward window were still filled with greenish, under-the-sea glass. 'Like the colour of your own mind,' Linet had said. He closed two panes that were open — the face and left side of the Blessed Virgin in one, the still head and massive shoulders of Gautama in another. 'Now you can see properly,' he said, wondering if Gwatkin appreciated his solution of various problems. But evidently this was not a region of experience where Gwatkin could navigate. 'It makes me think of the music I used to hear and the books I used to read,' he said. 'They're unexpected, those figures, those faces . . . high and frightening, like I used to think the gods were. The plants, too. As if gods had turned themselves into leaves. Perhaps everything one's brain tells one is impossible is true after all . . . even heaven . . . and you've seen it. Hell! I know what I want to say, but I can't.'

Well, it was satisfactory that his crowded windows — too crowded, he thought — had meaning, splendour, for someone in the world. Yes, too crowded. He must simplify.

'It's a damn funny thing,' said Gwatkin, 'how you are everywhere in your work.' Adrian and Mr. Pollock turned to hear what he said. 'Nobody else in the world, now or ever, would have done it. And yet it is super-personal, if that's a word.'

Mr. Pollock smiled and Adrian breathed a sigh. 'I shall soon be impersonal in my own life,' he said. 'I shan't exist, except as a means by which these gods and saints and flowers can manifest themselves.' Nice for Linet! He turned aside from the others and kissed the image of her that walked beside him. How strange, that she should be so real in the world, and these figures, gods and saints, so real in his own mind! For real they were, while he entertained them, living figures in the room with him. It was sad that they passed out of interest and became strangers, each one the incarnation, death, and tomb of an experience. But resurrection and ascension as well; for they lived, and on high. In what sense was this an experience? With what organ did Adrian understand pain, Adrian, who protected himself from imagination of suffering? The Madonna with her sweet thoughtful face and blue mantle; the Christ, golden-limbed, heavy with the pain of the world; the Buddha, lily-fleshed, terrible with annihilating thought, holy with the knowledge of his own end; Jehovah, aloof, big with judgment, throned above worlds; Jupiter in a blaze and the gods crowding — these were all things Adrian had lived, by some guess of imagination, and now lost. But even still, looking at his window, he recovered that longing, familiar in his boyhood, for the heavenly city, the daisied fields, the golden gates, angels lifting up their trumpets to blow them over the shining wall. There was the mild St. John and the stern Peter: one would like to think those beings existed in heaven, accessible to the prayers of men; and one day, perhaps, after that difficult mountain on which heaven stood had been ascended, visible to the eyes. There too the Archangel Gabriel, fair-haired and beautiful, with glittering sword and breastplate and sweeping wings. Adrian remembered that as a child he had wanted to be an archangel and suddenly appear from the nursery wardrobe, filling unjust nurse and parents with fear and remorse. How gratifying, when submitted to misinterpretation by petty natures, to spread wings with a fine look and leave the earth! No doubt that winged splendour in the window was himself. It was Adrian, too, grown-up, who now faced non-existence, with intent Indian face.

What if Linet should slip from interest and become a stranger; what if this experience also should die and rise again to live glassily in a window? He turned to the Reverend Eugene. 'I shall be asking you to marry us soon.'

Mr. Pollock looked as though it was a pity, but it was no use fighting against fate. 'The young man insists,' he said to Gwatkin. 'It were better if he became a monk.'

'The decree will be made absolute in May,' Adrian said. 'That is to say, in about eight weeks.'

'Eight weeks more of that monastic reclusion which so favours creative activity.' But the clergyman's face relaxed. 'God bless you, anyway, and your young lady, who, though fairylike and etherial in appearance, is equipped, I doubt not, with the means to answer your desire of her, and will probably give you a brood of mortal children. Well, well: it is not for me to speak, or put my thoughts into the course of human lives. For it is possible to hold that life is more than art.'

'I'm glad you think so,' said Adrian, as if re-assured.

10

LINET came home in May and stayed with the
Mansfields, who had returned from Argentina, in their
town house. Adrian asked Mr. Pollock if he would
marry them on the following Sunday. 'It occurs
to me that I ought to tell you,' he said, 'that we
are lovers already.'

'That was obvious,' Mr. Pollock replied. 'There
is a man in me that saw it with approval, as
according to robust, unchastened nature and in
the case of you two having an added comeliness.
It was, if I may say so with reverence, a union
decreed after the true pattern of holy marriages,
and I shall have no hesitation in sanctifying it, for I
believe it to be God's will.' The pale eyes looked
long at Adrian over the spectacles, regretfully,
as if God's will were particularly inscrutable in this
case. 'I add, with solemnity, that the sacrament is
holy, and it is God who marries you.'

'That is how I look at it,' Adrian inflexibly
replied.

'Knowing yourself and all that may come to pass
in you?'

'Knowing that it is in me to love one woman all
my life, and I shall do so.' Adrian felt a little
shiver pass through his body as if he had taken an
oath in the courts of heaven before the eyes of
Presences. Yet he wondered a little that this

clergyman, and Mr. Mansfield, and Linet herself, had their doubts of him; for he knew his love that it was simply himself and would die when he died in whatever world death came.

During those April mornings, when they opened the house once more to breezes from the garden and hyacinths grew in the window boxes, during those lengthening afternoons, those May nights heavy with expectation of unimaginable things, he adored Linet with some immortal part of him; and what he adored was like the beauty in daffodil, or bunch of new sticky lime-leaves, or bodiless beauty of some shape in the light itself, not subject to death. When they talked about their wedding his mind swayed and he felt a little faint, as at the vision of unreality. 'Can I take you straight home, after?'

'I think not,' she said. 'It would embarrass Bella.'

He smiled, recovering his sense of their relationship, for it was Linet, he saw, who would find it embarrassing. 'Well, then, we must have a honeymoon. A short one, because it will be beautiful to live together at home during May. Do you agree?'

'Yes.'

'Where shall we go?'

'I leave that to you.'

He saw a look in her eyes as she turned a little away. His answer came to him. 'The Luxembourg Gardens,' he said.

She flung herself into his arms. 'That was marvellous, Adrian darling, marvellous to hear you say what I hoped for!'

They were married, in the presence of two or three Mansfields, with lilies and music.

WHEN Adrian at last brought Linet home, on a
fine afternoon in June, Mark and Bella receded
from familiarity. They welcomed her with smiles
and much kindness; but Adrian, who thought he
understood them, was at a loss to know what their
feelings were. Possibly Mark dreaded her arrival
as the ending of a pleasant, thoughtful routine.
Possibly Bella, who temperately and with unspoken
reserves approved of Linet, foresaw usurpation,
or considered her an additional, useless member
of the family (for she would not think it useful to
be merely married to Adrian). Perhaps they both
felt that Adrian no longer needed friendship.
But it certainly seemed to Adrian that they retired
and became less friends than the after-representa-
tives of a dead generation.

Perhaps, he thought, sitting with the three of
them at tea under the holly-trees, Linet was right;
perhaps that was what she meant when she
said that his house was disagreeable to her in some
way, and he had quarrelled that time with a
strong dumb instinct in her. I will never do that
again, he said, repeating a vow made many times;
it is foolish to quarrel, and arises from a pride that I
will put an end to in myself; I will have infinite
patience, suffer all provocation and injustice without
answering, even if she twits me for that with being

indifferent, taciturn, or secret. I shall remember
that there has been some cause for it in myself
that I have not seen. For she is heavenly. He looked
across at her where she sat in her primrose frock
beside Bella, a little constrained; and he was filled
with passionate and protective affection. It might
well be practicable to move to some other house, at
least when he had put by some money, and retain
this one as a home for Mark and Bella, and as a
workshop. Not fair, perhaps, to have brought her
to a house so dense with past lives and experiences:
that was what oppressed her, doubtless. But he
loved it so much, and still hoped she would come to
feel with his own sense of it a special beauty in that
old-fashioned architecture of wall-space, column
and entablature, faulty as it was (and many faults
hidden by thick ivy). Better wait until she had
seen the alterations that were made for her, and had
a good chance to decide in her senses whether she
could like the mansion. After all, it was in that
greenhouse perched on stone in an angle between
the wings that they met.

There were letters, Bella remembered. She
fetched them, letters from Mansfields, with good
wishes. 'They are kind people,' Bella said, 'very
kind.' She often remarked on it if people were
kind, reassured perhaps to know there was kindness
in the universe.

'Oh Adrian!' Linet exclaimed. 'Viola's engaged!'

'No!' Adrian was astonished. So was Linet, as if
she had thought Viola would never be engaged

185

now. 'But then,' she said, using language that was always astonishing to Bella, 'It's best at any rate to try and have a satisfactory sex-life.'

'If I have understood you,' Bella said in her quiet voice, 'I don't agree.' But she did not wish, evidently, to expose her thoughts on this matter. 'Viola is probably very much in love,' she added presently.

'I hope not,' Linet said, and Bella glanced up. Adrian was thinking how sad it was that a Mansfield was going to marry and begin the dispersal of that loved family. 'I am not sure. . .' Bella began a sentence, and became blank. Adrian looked over at Mark and met his eye. They had seen that blankness too often lately. Adrian found himself turning away as if from fear of unnameable pain.

At an early moment Bella and Mark withdrew, leaving them the garden; disappeared into their own apartment, leaving them the house. Adrian took his wife indoors and led her from room to room, trying to make her see some beauty in light or shape or pleasurable collection of objects. She hung on his arm, listening, smiling, seeing beauties for herself. Presently they came to a small cosy room on the first floor overlooking the drive and shrubbery. 'This is for you,' Adrian said.

'For me?'

'Yes, when you want solitude.'

'I love it!' she said, enamoured of solitude at once. 'But how did you know I'd like this colour and these things?'

He grinned. 'Well, we did go a round of the shops

together, and you did tell me which things you liked best.'

'What a fool I am! I never guessed you were going to buy anything for me.' She stroked the beautiful smooth writing table, and the pale delphinium curtains, and a fine glass amphora within whose contours an altered room existed. There were flowers in the window, and salvinia with two or three red snails in a glass tank. 'You were excited about them one day,' Adrian explained.

'It was like you to get them,' she said. 'How well you know me! It's a kind of genius you have . . . sometimes.'

'If there's anything you don't like, it can be changed,' he told her. 'Or you can have everything new if you prefer some other scheme. I wanted to give you a surprise, so I chose things for you . . . after hearing what you liked, of course.'

'It's a wonderful present,' she said. 'It's marvellous to have a man choose for you and give you a house to live in.' She stopped and reflected a little. 'How terribly female I'm getting.'

He understood what she meant, and saw now perhaps for the first time how extensively it was true. 'Now come and see the bedroom,' he urged.

It was the bedroom that Mark's and Bella's parents had used, a long large room over the drawing-room with two fine windows. There was a dressing-room annexed. But Adrian had taken means to banish old presences: the occupants of an old stuffy room — containing marbled wash-hand-stand, massive wardrobe and dressing table, loaded mantelpiece and gilded mirror, frilled and becurtained mahogany bed and a wallpaper whose fading leaves and roses were hidden beneath landscapes in water-colour with tarnished frames — would never have recognized, had they been able to return, this monastic simplicity of oak and whitewash and bare polished floor; nor the sudden stark richness of curtains and bedspreads in gold and emerald; nor the sea-green bathroom through an open door on the left.

Linet looked round in silence, and now Adrian was terrified her strong and idiosyncratic taste would resent his not having consulted it. But he had consulted it: he knew it, or thought he did. Still, it was dangerous to have done this; foolish, perhaps, to have spent so much money on it (in the teeth of Gwatkin's protests). If she didn't like it he would spend as much again, and earn it afterwards! Linet was staring; but out of the window, not at the furniture; with a rapt face for all the world as if she made some renunciation. Then her attention was drawn to an object that crept round the door, a queer intelligent tawny creature with a black face, a Siamese cat, a crowning gift of insight and love on Adrian's part. Linet changed. Her looks became all delight, and falling to her knees she took the cat in her arms. Adrian watched with a sort of passionate pleasure.

'Is it new?' she asked, looking up at him over the cat's black face.

'New? Yes. I got him for you, to go with your sitting room. He ought to have been there, really.'

'Adrian!' She reached out a hand and pulled herself up. 'Sometimes you make me see your love almost with my eyes, and I feel then as if it could never change or die, and we are really married to make our life together. It's frightening to have seen so much and think we might fail.' She clung, and he comforted her, invincibly confident. 'And Adrian,' she said. 'Sometime shall we sleep in the tower?'

'To-night?'

'Yes.'

'To-night then. It would be right.' To-night she should invade his dearest privacy, as he had invaded hers, and he would be glad of it, as she was; and in the deep tide of his affection for her he felt no slightest disappointment that she had rejected, for to-night, this gift of their room. Presently she would possess it and make it answer her personality. There was space for her to turn cartwheels. He thought of it more as her room than his. 'Shall we spread out some of your things?' he suggested. She smiled, remembering their piggery in Antwerp, and he went downstairs for the suit-cases. It was strange, to walk upstairs and through the house with a suit-case in each hand, thinking of that delicate bright presence waiting for him at last in their own bedroom, thinking how all was changed. It was great happiness and contentment to be married. For an artist, he reflected, I am a remarkably conventional man. I wish . . . he stood still and looked down the corridor . . . I wish there were already some children running along here.

When he got back to the room, clothes were already scattered, for Linet, true to her nature, was preparing herself for a bath. He stood in the door. How this evening sunlight poured into the sea-green bathroom! How golden she was in the flood of it, and like a wave creature! He did not smile over it, because his thoughts were grave at the moment — would it be cruel to fill that fair belly with child and condemn her beautiful frame to the torture? 'Come on,' she said, 'I want my sponges and things. And then, if you don't mind, that other case with my evening frocks.' He fetched what she wanted, and between them they put away her clothes in the elegant plain wardrobe and chest-of-drawers, arranged bottles and brushes on shelves in the bathroom, disposed of her belongings, and his, in appointed places. Linet dressed, slowly, luxuriously, while Adrian in his turn took a bath. 'It is marvellous to have a home and be looked after,' she said, vigorously brushing her hair in the doorway. 'I never thought I should let anyone choose my surroundings. But you are clever, there are lights where there ought to be, and I like the way the bath fills.'

'I learnt that from the Ritz in Barcelona,' he explained. 'Do you remember that time?'

'Do I remember it!'

'Those cascades and trees of fire on the mountain? All those changing fire-shapes, and you saying that love especially was like that?'

A flash of that first Linet: 'What a fool one is to pretend anything else!'

'I never agreed with you,' he said. 'My instincts tell me something different.'

She watched him soberly: 'It would be terrible, now, to find it was true.'

Presently, while he was fixing his tie, Linet, astride a chair with her arms on the back of it and her chin on her arms, asked what frock she should wear.

'The green one.'

She rose, turned a cartwheel as he had foreseen, and fetched up between him and the mirror that filled the wall space between the two windows. She glanced at herself in the glass. 'Aren't I elegant? Why do you always like me in green?'

'Because you remind me of greenfly, my Inseck.'

'I'm not an inseck.'

Their exchanges, whether light or serious, were in the pattern of some other sustained conversation between them. They were in touch with each other profoundly; perhaps never so much in love as now. It gave them isolation, so that Bella and Mark, who were there at dinner, remained on the distant inaudible fringes of their world. The day lingered into marvellous evening. And up in Adrian's tower those two sat with hands clasped while the light of evening changed into the light of dawn.

THE first weeks of their marriage passed without any debasement of this immortal kind of reality. It was all strange to Linet. Bella refused to let her do the housekeeping, clinging to it, in spite of now too frequent suffering, as if to life itself; and Adrian wouldn't let her do any housework, in spite of Bella's opinion, unspoken but evident. Linet explained to Bella that she had done plenty of work in her time and wasn't afraid of it. 'But he won't let me,' she said. 'He thinks I'm a fairy, or something.'

'I know that, my dear,' Bella said. 'He's soft about you at present.' Linet smiled, wondering if Adrian would grow hard with her one day and make her do housework. She found it amusing, after a bit, to wander from room to room in the business part of the establishment, watching and asking questions. Mark, it was evident, thought her a plague. One day she turned up in an overall and demanded instruction in cutting, leading and staining. Adrian, when he heard of it, did not at first approve of her having anything to do with his work; but she looked so absorbed and so pretty, when he saw her fair hair bent over the litter of her experiments with the cutter, that his heart yielded.

One brilliant morning he came to her room with a letter and announced that he had been commissioned to do windows for the great new church, headquarters of a theosophical community in London. He was both elated and dissatisfied. 'It's a tremendous thing,' he said, hoping she would understand the importance of the event.

'Then why are you worried?'

'Partly because it's such a frightful opportunity, if you understand me.'

'I do. And partly what else?'

'Well, I shall have to think about God.'

'I feel clear about Him. I should know how to do Him, if I could draw.'

'Should you? You're lucky. The more I think the more positively I understand that I've no knowledge of Him whatever . . .' But Adrian withdrew his thoughts from exposure. 'Let's go for a little walk round the roads and enjoy the lime trees,' he suggested.

Linet was pursuing a train of thought and would not move until she had finished. Her eyes were fixed on the snails in their glass tank. Her lips moved slightly. Is it very good manners, he wondered, to insist on finishing one's thoughts there and then? It's very important to finish them, of course, and I know she is always right. But he tapped a little with his foot.

All at once her thoughts came visibly to an end. 'Yes,' she said, 'let's go for a little walk. Sorry I made you be impatient.'

'It's nothing,' he protested, all animosity subsiding, and they walked arm-in-arm under the lime trees.

'I should like to give a party,' she said presently.

'Well, of course! We met first at a party. Or didn't meet.'

'I used to look at you and think how marvellous it would be to know you.'

'And I thought you never gave me so much as a glance. Why didn't you make friends?'

'I don't know. Perhaps I thought it would be too dangerous.'

'Dangerous! Surely I look innocent enough!'

She laughed at him. 'And are you, my lamb?'

What had she been afraid of? He didn't quite like the picture she made of him. 'Well,' he said, 'We'll give a party. It will be fun.'

They planned like children, and gave their party at last on a hot summer night, with charades by candlelight on the terrace. A few heads looked out of windows. A policeman watched affably from the pavement, with a small crowd of strollers, or servants from neighbouring houses. Linet herself designed and rehearsed the charades, and Adrian saw with a shock of pleasure that she was creative. Her personality was fully manifested in those tableaux, by candlelight, between the glistening holly trees, as praying mantis with green and grisly limb, as youth with relentless eyes and prideful rapier, as fair snowy figure on a bride-cake, crowned with white leaves and icy roses. She was excited with her triumph, a little transfigured and unearthly — not to be touched, Adrian felt, though he wanted to kiss the crimson mouth in her pale-painted face. A man sitting in front of him on the grass watched with attention as she moved about afterwards in her bride-cake dress of stiff lace, a short gnome-like young man with broad shoulders, large spectacles and an intelligent forehead. An intellectual: Adrian saw it by the way he sat on the lawn, easily disposing his legs, almost in the Buddha-attitude. Yes, and though his eyes followed Linet about, it was (unlike Gwatkin's) without anxiety, without eagerness, if not quite with dispassion. Adrian addressed a remark to him: 'She did very well, didn't she?'

'Tolerably, tolerably. She is a little too much transported, don't you think? Too inspired, really. No?' The bright, intelligent eyes considered him through candle-reflecting lenses. I'll take this chap in presently to look at my sage, Adrian reflected. Linet came up just then. 'Oh, Tracy,' she said, 'do you know my husband? Adrian, this is Tracy Castlebridge, the explorer. Tracy, this is my husband.'

'Let's see,' the explorer replied. 'Who as a matter of fact is your husband? I seem to remember some other face.'

'Quite,' said Linet. 'His name is Adrian Douglas. He makes windows for churches.'

'It must be very bad for you,' Tracy observed.

'I'm not sure that it isn't.' Adrian was quite ready to agree. 'But there are windows besides church windows, you know.'

'Oh, perfectly. All I object to is this charging of

light with emotion. If you must do it, confine yourself, I do beg, to churches, where one needn't go.'

Now Adrian resented something in this small
man that was inimical to his whole activity.
But he knew himself to be weak in controversy,
like many artists; and in any case he was unwilling
for the self-exposure that controversy involves; he
refrained therefore from answer. Linet, who had an
inveterate passion for argument, looked disap-
pointed; but a swift glance to Adrian showed
that she accepted his reserve. 'Adrian,' she said,
'I want dancing. Will you chase them all in?'

Presently there were some thirty couples dancing
in the painted drawing-room, to music that streamed
from enchanted forests and regions beyond pelican-
haunted seas. Adrian danced with Viola: it was their
first meeting since her engagement. She was
flushed and lovely, sheathed in a long amber frock;
but silent. They were both silent. Adrian found
himself watching Gwatkin, who stood in a corner,
too shy to dance but envious of the dancers, especially the man who was dancing with Linet. Really,
it was difficult to find anything to say; and when
the dance was over Adrian was glad that Viola
accepted his proposal to join her parents for supper.

They sat down to a table. 'Yes, Viola will live
in Buenos Aires,' Mrs. Mansfield said. 'It's a long
way off and you can imagine that I am sorry. We
shall only see her once in three years.'

'It's a pity. You must hate it.'

'It's what happens, you know. They will all leave

us. I hope it, for their sakes. It's often sad for parents, I suppose.'

'But specially for you and your husband, who have loved your children, your family, so much. I'm terribly fond of them myself, if I may say so.'

She looked at him enigmatically. 'There will be some left for years yet, I'm glad to say.'

'At least,' said Adrian, 'it's a good thing for the world that children of yours should be scattered through it.'

She smiled and looked young. 'Thank you, Adrian.'

He saw Linet with Tracy and Gwatkin in a corner. Linet, with her frock of stiff lace, pulled up to her knees, listened with interest and pleasure to what Tracy said, and he said a good deal, between tankards of beer. It was remarkable, it was enviable, what he drank. He was still talking when everyone else had gone, and Gwatkin still listened. Adrian joined in.

'Your drawing-room wallpaper,' Tracy said at once. 'Emotional, romantic, fact-blinking.'

'You are not a profound man, I should think.' Adrian felt entitled to use the same frankness.

'Profound? Possibly not, if that means mystical. But accurate.' He filled a pipe, with the air of one who expects an intellectual treat.

'You remind me of a rum omelette,' Adrian said. 'High flames and a shallow dish.'

'I like you,' Tracy said.

'And I should say you are immensely selfish.'

197

Linet grinned catlike. Tracy, curling both legs on a chair so that he sat on his own feet, prepared to speak. When he began, the faint opening sentences of other people would be swept right away. 'Now this,' he said, 'is the stuff. No? This will be an evening.'

'Whose evening?'

Tracy ignored the interruption. 'That sage of yours, a mystic, a man suffering from the most ridiculous of illusions, that there is some God-knows-what in things, or behind things or where-ever it is in relation to things. Instead of just things. . .' He continued, with remarkable lucid-ity, considering what he had drunk. But Adrian did not follow many sentences. He recognized that this was a man without metaphysical sense. With-out sense of his own Being, perhaps. But why do I spell it in my mind with a capital? he asked himself; perhaps there is nothing to have sense of, and my sage and I myself are above all men deceived. He pondered. Gwatkin listened with all his attention, save what he used for glancing at Linet. Linet was listening too. How does a woman deal with such arguments within herself? Adrian wondered.

At last the man went. 'I don't think I much care for parties in my own house,' Adrian said, surveying remains. 'They are a kind of affront to one's privacy.'

'You *would* feel like that, darling.' Linet declined on his shoulder, all the life that had waxed so high in her now sleeping.

'Who is Castlebridge?' he asked, as she struggled out of her frock.

'I told you. An explorer. Interior of Brazil.' She stretched like a cat and yawned. 'We used to know each other when I was first married, and I met him in Brussels, when I was away . . . I'm very fond of him. He wanted me himself once.'

'Oh, did he!'

'Not to marry him. He says marriage is the extreme of human incompetence.'

'Oh, does he!'

She smiled at the tone in Adrian's voice with a last flare of her energy, and drooped off to brush her teeth.

TRACY and Gwatkin began to make themselves
quite at home. Now Linet was here, Gwatkin
grew less willing to play chess, and Mark betook
himself with contentment to his own quarters.
Gwatkin attended closely to what Tracy said,
glancing often at Adrian, as if he were making up
his mind between them. But on most evenings
Adrian left the three of them talking and went
to the tower and his books; for at this time he was
trying to absorb all modern knowledge, as if that
might bring him to the experience he wanted. The
task was certainly difficult. 'A lot of these damn
sciences are beyond me,' he said; but with the aid
of popular expositions he obtained the sense of
mathematical and scientific enquiry, and did not
perceive that in the dissection of phenomena
something escaped. He studied ethics and theology;
and here one thing stuck in his mind, namely,
that several writers said no man still bound by his
senses could see God — a threat to Adrian in his
art and in his life. It was the more poignant when
he crept through the house and found Linet asleep,
with her clothes neatly folded on a chair, the
tangled crown of her head alone visible above the
sheet.

Linet was unpunctual, and Adrian, unartistlike
in so many ways, preferred to do everything on the

stroke. She told him one morning when she was late for a luncheon appointment that 'time was made for slaves.'

'That,' he replied, 'like so much of the wisdom of the ages, is incorrect. A man is a slave unless he accepts time.'

'Well, I shall always take as much time as I like.'

'Precisely. And miss the bus.'

For a moment they looked at one another with leaping antagonism. It was Linet who suddenly relaxed, and said 'I should like to go to the opera to-night. It's *La Bohême*. Could we?'

'I'll go and book a couple of stalls,' Adrian said, forgetting his misgivings about the life of the senses.

'You'll do nothing of the sort! Gallery for us.'

'Gallery your eye! Sitting on three inches of board in a crowd of sweaty Italians all pushing with their backs and their knees.'

'I like Italians. You're getting middle-aged and luxurious, Adrian. You've lost your taste for the simple things. . . .'

'I never had it,' he put in.

'. . . and all you want now is rich food, boiled shirts and stalls and cigars. Like an ox.'

'Oxes don't have cigars,' he pointed out, 'or boiled shirts.'

'And you'll soon cease to create.'

This argument filled him with alarm; he planned for himself a course of hardship. 'It's true we're hard up,' he said. 'Gwatkin says so. Gwatkin has become a sort of speaking purse: I put my hand in and it says No. We'll go balcony.'

'Gallery,' she said.

She stood firmly with hands clasped behind her, most pleasing to see.

'All right; gallery.'

She was delighted. 'We'll go and pin our names on camp-chairs: there's a man looks after them.' They did so, and as Adrian had an appointment in town, and Linet had someone coming to tea, they arranged to meet at six-thirty outside the opera-house and look for something to eat. At six-thirty Adrian was there: Linet was not. She turned up at ten minutes to seven, nervous. 'I really couldn't help it,' she said, looking at his face. 'The water wouldn't get hot for some reason, and you wouldn't expect me to come without a bath.'

He hid from her that the idea had crossed his mind.

'Dirty and in the clothes I've worn all day,' she went on.

He did not remark that she would still be clean in clothes worn a month.

'And you know what the Tube is like,' she said.

Adrian, who by now was clenching his hands, did not mention that he had come by Tube himself. There are always excellent reasons why a person is late, he thought.

'And it makes me feel awful to know I'm keeping

you waiting and you're getting irritated. Why on earth didn't you go and sit on a camp-stool, when you know how it makes me feel.'

It seemed a reasonable question, but it made him angry. He managed to say, with an air of mild acceptance, 'I rather like standing, I don't mind waiting and I'm not irritated. Don't bother yourself in the least, my dear.'

She smiled inscrutably and took hold of his arm. 'Let's go and get dinner.'

'But there isn't time for dinner. The man won't keep our seats much longer.'

'There is, and he will.'

'Very well.' Adrian marched off, setting his jaw. He could see that his face annoyed her, and he couldn't help it; he was only trying to control his own temper. Hell! They should have been so happy! Why couldn't she bend a little?

Suddenly Linet pulled her hand away from his arm, and stopped dead in the middle of the pavement. 'Adrian! I'm irritating you beyond bearing. Would you rather leave me and go by yourself? I'll go home.'

He answered with intensity, trying to burn up and abolish this fantastic antagonism by sheer power of will. 'I want only to go with you, Linet; I want nothing else, and I want it very much.'

When he had said this he saw it was actually true, and that impulse to accept her suggestion and get rid of her was an impulse of anger, flimsy and as it were non-existent.

She considered his answer.

'Do you believe what I say?' he asked, surges of pride still washing his brain.

'Yes.' She spoke in a neutral tone. Linet once driven away from herself could not easily return. But she was mollified, pleased. He knew it, and had patience. 'I don't mind if we miss some of it,' he said. 'Or even if we have to stand.' He hoped she wouldn't think he meant to say it would be her fault if they did.

'I mind,' she replied, sharply but with a side-glance; and he knew that she only ventured this last acerbity because peace was on the way to be made between them. He rejoiced. 'Let's eat here,' she suggested.

They went in where she pointed, and enjoyed sandwiches, coffee, and cake. 'I'm sorry you didn't get a proper dinner,' she said, soft as butter, as they strolled back. 'We can have a picnic when we get home.'

'It's a matter of perfect indifference to me.' Adrian lied handsomely out of his passionate affection for her; and Linet accepted it. But she was never really deceived.

When they got back their camp stools were still reserved. It was not in Linet to express triumph. They waited for the gallery doors to open in great content with each other, glancing back, now and then, like people who have escaped from danger.

They experienced the music, the superb singing of the tenor, as if they were one person. It was delicious to see Linet, in her pretty frock, flushed and tense, her eyes glowing like a leopard's, ready to pounce from her high place in the darkness on those people in that lit space far below. She was alone with Adrian, bright and cool in that sweating crowd; she belonged to him; she had no mind for anything but the music and her lover, he and it inseparable.

As for Adrian, he gave himself up, after some minutes of inward conflict, to the splendour of night and music, the miracle of their passion.

THAT reconciliation was not complete; important parts of their natures were not involved. Fortunately, they were soon to go to the Mansfields who had once more taken the château. It was time for a holiday. Adrian, labouring in the tower, among the tops of silent, August-heavy trees, would find his attention easily taken by the tapping of a hammer, the hum of a mowing machine, or sudden aspiration of leaves in a breeze. Sometimes, if he looked out of the window, there would be Linet going hatless down the road, with her shopping basket and her Siamese cat, stopping perhaps to stare at something, to tease a dog, or to meditate. She enjoyed her solitude in the mornings, he thought. She seemed far away from him down there in the road, receding, vanishing round a corner. He leaned on the window-sill, heart-smitten because of a sudden insight of her loneliness.

Certainly she was difficult, unforeseeable, easily put out, oppressed, driven away: a very few weeks of experience proved it. It was wonderful that she had escaped the crushing forces of the world with nothing to oppose to them but her unearthliness. She was daring and fearful at the same time, like a child; ready to act on imagination, like a child; unappalled by dangers that the sophisticated would not face, frightened only by terrors the sophisticated have never seen. She seemed to accept the facts of the world, more facts indeed than most people bring themselves to look at; in particular the truths of her own experiment. She was experimental, by resolve, because she thought it was good for her. She married Carl by way of experiment: at least, it was agreeable to Adrian to think so. After the collapse of her marriage she had taken a lover for experience because body and mind inclined her thereto as desirable and reasonable. And it was for loneliness and because she suffered, he added, by way of explanation to his own feelings. She learnt to pity men, to despise them, to admire their ruthlessness, and to envy their position of initiative. She had constructed a world that should be satisfactory to live in, for a sensible person; and now it was difficult to be sensible because she was possessed by what she had dreaded, passion for a man, who knew her; love that flowed to the farthest parts of her body and lived in her as her soul.

Adrian turned his head quickly from side to side, looking for some escape over the roofs and tree-tops. He had a responsibility. He looked down to the drive, and his eye fell on that greenhouse in the angle. Sparrows were hopping on the brown earth among shrubs. A queer thought came into his head: I'll build her an aviary. Why on earth should that thought come into my head? Do I want to appease her, because I spend so much time up here thinking about things and working? Am I just whistling to the bird I have driven away?

Oh well! It was necessary to work. But he kept on going to the window, and at last saw Linet returning, with her arms full of parcels and flowers. He ran down and went out of the gate to meet her. She was pleased when she understood that his thoughts had been towards her.

In the afternoon he took her to Hampton Court, and she showed pleasure in the water-lilies, the ducks, and the dense vegetation by the stream; but she came not quite back to him from the far-off region where her spirit had gone that day. Gwatkin and Tracy had invited themselves to dinner: 'one of the few private houses where I get things properly iced,' Tracy remarked. There are always restaurants, Adrian replied in his head; but you're one of those people who feed free. Tracy was quite capable, he knew, of sustained starvation. He had done it in South America, Linet said. Adrian didn't quite understand why Linet usually lit up when Tracy came. The fellow certainly had something in him. . . .

As soon as dinner was over she went off to attend to Bella, who was confined to her room. The three men sat on the terrace. It was bad luck for Linet that there should be a sick woman to look after; pity if Bella symbolized for Linet something disagreeable in the house. Perhaps that was the cause of Linet's oppression.

'God?' Tracy raised as it were an eyebrow at the naïve question — it was Gwatkin's. He had a disarming mouth, you might say; it grinned widely.

208

He was, in fact, an amiable fellow, and showed no objection (if he still wanted Linet himself) to Adrian's having her. He beamed, and sat on his feet, and talked, and drank with large tolerance anything that came his way. 'If Linet had only taken to drink,' he said, 'she wouldn't be so damn choosey.' He lifted his glass to Adrian. It was a sort of acknowledgment. 'As to God. What hope is there for men in any reasonable idea of God? And what reasonable idea is there of God? Let us make up our minds that at death the theatre that we call an ego ceases to afford the opportunity for spectacle; the collection of activities that we are is dispersed. We may therefore live by our own standard of values. As to science, it is nothing but the negation of hope. Except for soda-water syphons, its principal achievement. Science simply affords the prospect of the continuous extinction of what is in what follows; with a final extinction of the last results in nothing. There is thus no object in activity, except to gratify some desire; and it is pure illusion to suppose that by the cessation of desire there is to be attained some state of blessedness. I myself have reduced my desires to a few main ones that I can gratify easily; food and drink, that are abundant if one cultivates the right friends; women, who afford no singular difficulty if one avoids, by a cultivated instinct, those afflicted with ideas; and I can sleep on a tub. One likes continuous newness. . . .'

Gwatkin, taking advantage of the pause while

o   209

Tracy was swallowing, asked 'What about love, though?' and at once looked as if he wished he hadn't.

Tracy banged his quart tankard on the table with the air of one who is ready to put in another hard spell. Adrian went off to refill the tankard from a barrel that he kept in the cellar; when he returned Gwatkin looked as if he was moved in some way. 'In short' (Tracy used this phrase as a kind of conjunction for coupling large volumes, and by no means to preface abbreviation), 'love is not a function proper to the male, but to the female, and if a man is capable of prolonged affection for a woman, or if he dotes on children, he is three parts feminine.'

Adrian reflected on his own case. 'You require to go further into things,' he said. 'You haven't thought far enough. You don't know things.' He registered, as it were, a formal protest, wondering at the same time what it was that he knew himself; and Tracy's ideas sank in. 'I see your trouble,' he continued, catching glimpses of an answer. 'You confuse femaleness and the psyche. You don't even know that the psychic constitution of men and women is profoundly different.' He spoke from the book.

'The psyche?' Tracy gleamed benevolently through his spectacles. 'The psyche? A thing found in savages.'

'You have no feeling of existence perhaps! Not even your own? Your psyche has merely died;

this is a modern calamity. Whereas my sage has understood the psyche with his intellect, submitted his intellect to it. He has united life and consciousness.' But Adrian experienced division within himself even as he spoke.

'Love follows always the same pattern,' Tracy was saying. 'I hate the ridiculous gestures of lovers. I laugh at myself when I find myself using them. That stretching out of the neck. That pursing of the lips. . . .'

Adrian began a long argument within himself. 'One gets over the habit of love as one gets over biting the nails,' Tracy was saying.

Two or three days later Linet fell into a misery.
Adrian devoted himself to her (with an occasional
glance tower-wards, for urgent problems awaited his
thoughts), but could find no means of rescue. He
tried his utmost to discover by reflection the cause
of her trouble. Was there anything he had said or
done; or not said, or not done? At lunch she was
taciturn, resentful, as if perhaps Bella and Mark
were the representatives, at that feast, of all that
troubled her. Or Adrian himself: perhaps these
family luncheons were a mistake, and it would be
better if they lived somewhere else and he went off
to his work in the mornings like other men.

After lunch he asked her what she would like to
do. 'Work,' she said, and presently he met her
gliding sulkily along the passage in her overall. It
seemed best to let her get on with it; but Adrian
was dissatisfied, and after half an hour's laborious
and unfruitful designing he went to the cutting
room. She had spoiled a good deal of glass. 'I'd
like to talk to you,' he said. She looked up, with an
air as if talking might be about as useless as everything else. 'Let's go to the tower,' he said, and led
the way, boiling a little: after all, most people might
well think she just wanted smacking. She sat in
the window, stiffly; and he thought, why can't
you relax and lie there as you used to do, and I

should love your honey-coloured hair and the sweetness of you inside your overall!

It seemed best to be direct, even if that were to bring on a crisis. 'What's the matter, Linet, dear'?

'Do you expect me to know?'

'Well, I thought you might have an idea.'

'I have. Several ideas.'

It sounded ominous, and he brought himself to a question: 'Are you out of love?'

'You must be a fool to ask that.'

This was satisfactory, in one way at least. 'I dare say I am,' he replied. 'One is that sort of fool in love.'

'One is altogether a fool, in love. Handed over body and soul to the will and mercy of someone else.'

'I don't want you to be at my will and mercy. I don't want to possess you, any more than I want to be possessed.'

He could have enlarged on this theme; but it touched her where she was suffering. 'You keep me out of your real life. You pen me up in a house I don't like, so that I can be handy when your work that really holds you is done. You didn't even let me choose what my own room was to look like.'

Adrian was profoundly offended. She had been storing that up then. 'That's a rotten thing to say!'

'Why! Isn't is true?'

They sprang apart and watched one another like tigers; but some angel in the room reminded them of their vows. An unseen hand stroked all fury from Adrian; tears welled from Linet's under-lids and rolled down her nose. They held each other, shivering.

'I don't know what comes over me,' she said, 'or why it suddenly turns to a feeling like hate.' It was safe to say things like that now, for their emotions were somehow depotentialized.

'Same with me,' Adrian replied. 'We should be wicked if we gave way to it.'

'It's partly because I'm a woman. It's rotten to be a woman, and be the slave of your body. Not that men aren't. They're slaves of their stomachs. And other things.'

'Not all of them.'

'Oh, don't you think you're any sort of Indian saint, all detached from your senses! Yet! And you're not to be.'

She was yielding; she was returning; he used all his powers to entice her. 'It was true what you said earlier,' he put out. 'I did make you live here, simply because I so loved the house myself. I did choose what the rooms should be like; though I thought it would please you.' She did not seem to be listening: he braced himself. 'And if you like we'll go somewhere else.'

She pressed her breast against his and threw back her head to look at him. 'Really! Could we really go and live in Paris, in Montparnasse, somewhere high up looking over the Luxembourg Gardens?'

Hell! Everything is possible, somehow! 'Yes,' he said.

'Sweet idiot!' She was radiantly Linet for an instant; and, though the next instant she was almost gone again, Adrian felt an immense relief. Her next words were surprising. 'How are you getting on with your thoughts about God?'

'Not very well. I always find myself thinking about Krishna, Siva, or Vishnu, that I've been reading about.'

'May I look?'

First he showed her geometrical designs, abstractions. She looked and said nothing, and he felt a chill of misgiving. Then, rather unwillingly, he showed her designs from a portfolio, lion incarnations tearing kings to pieces, daemons, ascetics, gods rising in the darkness of trees by night, and innumerable flower patterns. They were flowing, vital, and mysterious. 'Of course, I've derived them,' he said.

'They're not derived,' she said. 'You're a bit Indian, else I don't see how you could have so much feeling for these subjects.'

'I suppose my soul still projects gods and daemons; and I've inherited somehow a stiff dose of Indian unconsciousness, or consciousness, or whatever it is; something perhaps that once knew Krishna. I must get away from all that. Look here.' He held it out to her as if he distrusted it, a design of Krishna and Radha in summer-night darkness among trees of unearthly pattern and mysterious life. 'This won't do for a window,' Adrian explained. 'It would be misunderstood.'

Linet exclaimed 'Oh! You must never get away from this. This is real you.' She checked herself, as if not daring to give advice. 'This is you and me,' she corrected. 'What marvellous foliage you've given us! What a beautiful flower border!' Adrian saw that she had understood his symbol of their union; his condensation of all splendour and ecstasy in the flower out of heaven that the god and his consort held in their passionate lily-hands. He perceived that a miracle had taken place and they were wholly restored to one another. He was contented, for the moment, with that, and accepted his own work.

Waiting for her that night in the window-seat of the tower he stared out at the summer-haunted trees. No gods appeared in the darkness of the trees, but a thought walked like a presence in the forests of his mind. When Linet came Adrian made her sit there beside him.

'Do you desire a child?'

'Yes.' She looked like a spirit.

'I too.'

She thought a long time. 'It will change things somewhat,' she said at last. 'But I'm ready for them to change.'

'It's the next thing for us.'

She looked deeply at him, as if wondering what was in his words. Then she accepted them. 'In France then. In Diane's bed.'

ADRIAN gave himself up to Linet for the time. Mark had promised to take care of Bella and they were off to France. It was wonderful to be crossing the Channel, boarding the train at Calais with sandwiches and grapes in their hands, spending the night at their favourite hotel in the Rue du Fleurus where they could crane out over the little iron balcony and stare at the trees in the Luxembourg Gardens; to be rushing to the Terminus Montparnasse after early breakfast, getting out on the platform at Chartres to see the towers of the cathedral, eating lunch in the train, finding again a certain heavenly happiness that seemed part of this scene, like the woods and the fields. And now they were at Saumur, in broiling heat, and Andrew was waiting with Marigold and Frances — but not Viola. Viola was married and gone to Buenos Aires. It made a gap and a sadness, as if someone had cut down a tree. Adrian resented her absence, as they drove along by the shoaly gleaming Loire, reach beyond reach; an element was missing from Paradise, as if they had taken away the woods from those hills on the farther bank, or the château from Amboise, or some tenderness from the wide, river-reflected sky.

But this was a distant, peripheral want; only felt because the completeness of that family, and Viola herself, had been part of his first experience here with Linet, two years ago. Two years ago! This thought led Adrian to guess at, and presently to perceive, other changes, changes within himself.

But for the moment he was taken up with the arrival. Once more they turned sharp right in the village of Faye la Vineuse and brought up before gates. The gates were opened by a polite man in leggings who wanted shaving. The gravel crunched under their tyres, and once again Andrew swept round and drew up at a front door surmounted by crown and salamanders. River and meadow and wood, those antique houses glimpsed over that further bridge, and a villager fishing in a punt at the bottom of his back yard, the stables, the vinery where lizards darted, plane trees and huge August flowers — everything was here. And the château itself! Adrian would not look at it until he could see it all at once and quietly. But its perfection was at the edge of his senses as a presence of which he was afraid.

In the meantime there was a crowd of Mansfields: Mick in a perambulator, Simone, and Michel who greeted Linet with a kind of sardonic ardour.

'Glad to see you. How are you?' Mr. Mansfield obtained knowledge of their state of mind in regard to each other with one robust diving glance. 'It's nice to have you here married and happy.' He announced their happiness as a fact to which they were to adhere. How far was Mr. Mansfield responsible for their marriage? Had he persuaded them to church in the interests of Linet's happiness? Did he trust her, then, with Adrian? Adrian always felt that Mr. Mansfield still reserved judgment about him. Oh well! It was so with him that he now minded a good deal less than he used to do what people thought of him. Linet had furthered his progress towards self-containment with the strongest evidence of her own approval.

'Are we to have Diane's room?' she asked.

'You are.' Mr. Mansfield smiled at her in great kindness. 'We've filled it with flowers for you.'

There was a little solemn moment between them. 'I owe you so much happiness,' she said.

Diane's room was indeed filled with flowers, great August flowers from a sultry garden, brown and golden and red, with strong green foliage. The furniture, the tapestries, the chairs and footstools, the bed, were old and rich and perhaps a little ghostly. This was agreeable to Adrian's disposition: his consciousness woke to old scenes as to a voice. Linet held him a minute, and whispered: 'It's lovely to have you here. Last time I was alone in this room and I wanted you. And in a way I didn't, because it was beautiful to be with my own secret self at night. I understand perfectly, Adrian, when you want to be like that. I had marvellous thoughts here by myself.'

He replied: 'I wondered if you would wish to admit me here.'

She asked: 'Have I not given myself to you?'

He wondered if this were not too much giving,

219

and reflected that she yet remained most unknown to him.

'And Selena is to be born here,' she said; 'born, I mean, into my body.' Already she called their child Selena; it was to be a girl. That seemed queer to Adrian, when he remembered what she so often said about women and men.

She behaved with sobriety all the time they were there, as if the child were already shaped in her heart. This was not the Linet who once crawled through a window and dropped into the pool from the limb of a tree, who dived from high places on the bank of the river, or galloped bare-back on a big chestnut mare about the park. She preferred, when they were not driving to Saumur, or Angers, or Chenonceaux, to lie and float in the warm river, or in a vineyard, or stretched out on the baked stone parapet of the terrace, as if it were August that should get her with child. They went to Loches, to Chinon, and many a field or wood where they had been peaceful, and found peace still there as if it were the substance out of which scene after beautiful scene had been conjured into existence. Adrian was content to be idle. Work seemed an impertinence on the part of man. All problems were in abeyance; not resolved, but in abeyance, waiting for a future that though only a fortnight away seemed infinitely remote. Life, other life, seemed merely relative to life here, to the perfection of being for which the château itself stood as sign. And Adrian knew that he had received a portion of that quietness, for the time, until he should perhaps throw it away.

It amused him to watch some of Linet's ways. In the daytime she wore a swimming suit, or an old cotton frock, or perhaps her pyjamas on very hot afternoons; but at night she produced rich effects, appearing in lilac, in violet, in green, in orange, in unnameable colours. With each she wore some appropriate necklace, of amber, crystal, moonstone, coral, jade and the like; and jewels that she had from her mother. It was amusing to see the affection that Millicent, the maid detailed to attend Linet, lavished on these dresses, these elegant shoes and simple silk underclothes, and her mute astonishment at the daytime garments, the cotton frock, the cotton vest and knickers, neat but mended. The others were charmed at Linet's ritual and lived up to it, so that it was sumptuous to dine under the carved and painted ceiling of that royal dining-room, to dance in the gilded salon with girls in delicate frocks, to play cards and eat supper on the terrace with candles that never flickered in the drowsy August night; and everyone felt as if Linet were a princess, royal in some way, and dedicated.

Sometimes, when they had all said 'good night' and the château was silent, Linet and Adrian would emerge in their pyjamas from a door in the corner-turret, cross the terrace, skirt the lily-thick lake, and make for the deep, whispering country. Once, returning, they came to the river, and Linet, warm-fleshed from the tawny moon, made her way through the reeds and Adrian followed her and they floated home on the current.

And one night they were held for a long time spell-bound by the château itself, and Adrian saw in that perfection the type of a perfected spirit that unites within itself all parts, all opposites, is passionless, released and without necessity. He saw, and envied.

AUTUMN and winter were full of labour for Adrian.
He was ashamed nowadays of his earlier work, and
tried now to produce something that should make
people forget it. On a bitter March day, rather in
two minds because of what Tracy had said about the
windows in Mr. Pollock's library, he took Tracy to
see Mr. Winterbotham's insectarium. But he had
recently modified his work in a way that Tracy
might well approve; there would come opportunities for him to see it. They were invited to lunch.
There were present — Mr. Winterbotham, Mr.
Pollock, two biological young men, Tracy, Mark
and Adrian.

Tracy had much to say, and Mr. Pollock looked
at him with the tolerance of one who knows that
there must be many kinds of men and all have
their destiny. 'I don't know what we are to see
this afternoon,' Tracy said, 'but I hope it will be
more agreeable to a realist intelligence than what I
was shown in this gentleman's library.'

'What has the intelligence to do with it?' Adrian
enquired. 'And what, is real?'

Tracy beamed at this beautiful opening. 'I reply
with the second part of your question. What, in
your scheme of things, is real?'

'The real is what has meaning.' The biological

223

young men looked startled. Tracy put down a glass of hock. And Adrian suddenly doubted himself.

'Truth is a private possession, eh?' Mr. Winterbotham asked it.

'Something that possesses private persons, I should have said. Something indubitable but inarguable.' Adrian scanned Mr. Winterbotham, a sententious man with a beard who left his face in the air, so to speak, when he had used it for a question. Adrian was not at all afraid of this eminent rich man, or of those doubtless brilliant young men of science who seemed to be schoolboyishly hugging some joke with reference to the great entomologist; but he did not much want, nowadays, to be called on for exact statement. Mr. Pollock watched him with sad, affectionate eyes.

Mr. Winterbotham tried to bring in the silent Mark. 'You are an artist, sir, as well as a renowned archæologist. Have you discovered that truth is beauty?'

Mark disclosed a mouthful of fish. 'I don't occupy myself with such questions, sir.'

'Oh!' Mr. Rutherford remained polite. 'Your time, I presume, is fully taken up with practical labours, like my own?'

Tracy found opportunity. 'It is for men in that predicament, I suppose, that a sort of potted philosophy, a philosophy of epigrams and pithy statements, was invented. It certainly couldn't flourish without them. As I was going to say. . .'
And he discussed. Adrian was pleased with him

224

for his cheek; not so the Winterbotham, who expedited the cutlets, and the sweet, and the cheese, and remarked while there was still a sound of the crunching of celery that the light would fail early. He said: 'We'll have coffee served in the apartment that we are here to inspect.'

They found the apartment surprising. It was the result of a struggle between Winterbotham, the architect, and Adrian in which Adrian had won, handsomely. He had indicated to the architect how he might satisfy Winterbotham's admitted requirements and provide the necessary space for his own operations: it was for the architect, he had said, to apply himself, after that point, to the purely architectural problems. The architect did so, but it was Adrian who dictated the terms, and Adrian who furnished the windows, the decorations and the little theatres where insects enacted their cycles in an appropriate light. Now he stood looking at his own work in the usual mood of disillusion, with something extra thrown in because he missed Linet. And was it strange, now she was withdrawn and preoccupied with an unseen life, as he often with visions, that he should long for her again with April passion?

This is too rich, he thought. It had been necessary to relate the glass to the wall-space by some intervening pattern; he had invented a foliage, therefore, a foliage transplanted from some mysterious forest of the mind; and it seemed to him at this minute a thought too strange. And as to the windows — he

P   225

remembered too much of the problems that had been involved. He had achieved solutions by special rhythms in the shape of the leaded panes, and in the framework. 'I wish now,' he observed to the clergyman, 'that I had been more abstract.'

'Have you become infected with the views of your talkative friend?' The clergyman sighed. 'If you are going to become abstractive, formal . . . how great are the dangers that threaten the human soul! And I thought you were talking good sense at lunch, though there were hesitations. . . .'

Quite a crowd of people arrived, and Adrian listened to the usual congratulations that always seemed late, as if they should have come when he first had his idea before ever it was worked out. 'What colour!' people said. 'I think there is too much,' he replied. Still, it was interesting that the glass had this effect on people that everyone found it mysterious. Here seven fierce-eyed fish loomed in a presence of reed-stalks. There, green flags with jewel-violet flowers ringed a pool. Some glittering water-beetle, creation of Adrian's inner mind, displayed wide gauzy wings and slimy purple back in a pattern of lilies and brown shade. Shape of hippopotamus with hooded eye floated in a rhythm of spear-blade leaves. A python, a marvel of jewel-glass, coiled in a darkness of its own nature. Each scene arose in its place, related to another by intervening pattern of abstract shapes or painted foliage. It was organic, a whole; people had the impression that they were enclosed within the visions of some exotic spirit. Yes, it is extravagant, Adrian said to himself; I should like to reduce it to rhythm and nothing else. He saw how it could have been done. It was a nuisance that he couldn't immediately get away to his room in the tower — stopping to kiss Linet on the way up.

Tracy was in full discussion, with glowing face and beaming spectacles. He drifted near to Adrian, in the company of two remarkably good-looking young women. 'Yes, I call this stuff religious,' he was saying. 'It's the same thing, really, as arch-angels, virgins, and so forth. Oh, quite; the intelligence has been used, certainly. But it's dream-stuff; the fantastic output of a primitive unconsciousness, rather creepy, and of no interest, except as a curiosity, to an intelligence that has released itself from the primitive.'

Adrian intervened. 'Precisely! A poor, thin, disembodied, unsupported intelligence.' He did not realize how near he was coming, on the path of his own fate, to a separation of parts within himself.

'Oh!' said Tracy. 'Did I introduce? This is the artist, the glassworker. His name's Douglas. Mine's Castlebridge — Tracy Castlebridge.' The young women looked interested in Adrian; but Tracy at once harnessed their attention. 'He talks about meaning. I don't know what that is, unless it's the vagueness of things that are still awaiting examination by the intellect. Something that vanishes when you turn on the light. A kind of green blur. All this.'

'I begin to agree with you.' Adrian smiled, but his mind was teased as if there were something he couldn't remember. One of the young women gave him an exceedingly favourable glance.

Tracy plucked her back to himself, so to speak. 'I don't know what your name is' — he seemed to reprove her for it— 'but I'm sure you'll understand when I say that it's obnoxious to interrupt the light with this sort of coloured shapes.'

'I don't in the least agree with that,' Adrian said. 'There may be argument as to the shape of the shapes. . .' But once again he felt as if he had forgotten something; there was a blight on his spirit. This was to be explained for the moment by physical changes: the light was going, the glass visions were whitening, fading, like a dying consciousness. One or two people arriving said there was heavy snow. It grew dark. That ended the consideration of Adrian's work, and the visitors turned their attention to the insects in their little theatres. Adrian was compelled to talk with several people, saying to himself with strange anguish, I want Linet!

Mr. Pollock asked if he might come home with Adrian to tea. Tracy asked himself as well, and extended a cheerful invitation to the two young women, who accepted. They walked home through changed, white-carpeted roads; the house with its yellow lights and snow-topped tower looked Christmas-cardy; snow lay on cornice and window-sill, and snow-flowers were growing up among the dark leaves of the shrubs in the drive. They had dining-room tea, with silver teapot, sugar basin and hot-water-jug, hot buttered scones in china bowls, bread-and-butter and jam, and a chocolate cake on a silver cake-dish. Bella being confined to her room, Linet presided over the steaming tray. She was quiet, remote, and flushed with a strange beauty; and Adrian was taken with profound sadness, for she was so different from the swift, darting Linet that it seemed as if the hand of Death had already withdrawn her to the next world, the next world where she really belonged. Death! This dreadful distance; then extreme separation! It was curious how Adrian longed for her when he couldn't have her, with emotions oddly intensified. A lump rose in his throat now, and tears were hot in his eyes. He thought he would be stifled and his heart would split with the grief of the thought of her decease. Then he perceived that Mr. Pollock was looking at him. They were a tea-party within a tea-party, those three — Linet removed and dedicate, Adrian watching her, their friend watching them both like a wry guardian angel.

After tea Linet went off to sit with Bella; and Adrian, when the visitors had at last gone, went to his room where he meant to work out what was in his mind. It was two hours before he admitted that it wouldn't go. His thoughts turned again and again to Linet. She possessed his mind, Linet and a vast melancholy. Why did she go off to sit with

Bella? Why did he neglect her; care for her and at the same time neglect her? He had not failed in thoughtfulness or patience during her pregnancy, even when she was most difficult. He saw now that it wasn't enough, without understanding wherein he had been deficient. Could I have spared more time? Could I perhaps have neglected my work? He made himself satisfactory answers to these questions without solving some profound and obscure puzzle. He rose and went through the house, and found Linet in the bedroom. It was dark in there, but he could descry her by the window with her nose and mouth pressed against the glass, looking out at the snow. 'Linet,' he said, and moved and put an arm round her. But she remained staring out at the snow on lawn and terrace and the snow that gathered in the grip of the holly-leaves. After a few moments he experienced a curious resentment, and withdrew his arm. He had sought her in love and she might have given him some acknowledgement.

'What do you want?' He knew by her voice that he had somehow driven Linet away: his heart sank.

'I wanted you,' he replied.

'You don't show it much.'

'I don't understand.'

'It's a long time since you gave me flowers. I would have liked snowdrops, or Christmas roses.'

'It's not a long time, it's a week.' That could not be the real cause of her aloofness. Adrian coped with anger that he felt spreading through and taking possession of him. Don't be proud and a fool, he said to himself. Think that she must be right and you wrong, though you don't yet know why.

'I suppose you think I'm just an exacting woman, demanding presents?'

'No. I don't think anything of the sort. Don't attribute thoughts to me. . . .' He stopped. How easily patience ran out!

'It's a pity,' she went on, 'that one should ever think life has any meaning. Tracy is right.'

'I think he talks simple rot,' Adrian said.

'You don't face facts. An artist should not fall in love. All he needs is solitude, especially at night, and to have a girl in his bed sometimes, and send her away when he's done with her. And if the girl's fool enough to fall in love with him that's her look-out, and he should just be remorseless.'

'I don't know what you're getting at,' Adrian answered. 'All this may be true about lots of people, but it's not true about me. I love you. I came to you just now because I loved you. What's the matter?'

She did not say. Probably, he thought, she couldn't say. It was damned irrational! He could see she was preparing some sharp reply; and she turned to him with hard, argumentative face. His own face went hard. He felt love drain from it, leaving a mask. Their eyes met in anger, strange anger. What was this anger that they had for each other that one or the other had warded off several

231

times already even during her pregnancy when it would be so terrible to quarrel; this hatred — one must use crude, accurate words — that sometimes lived in them and made them want madly to hurt each other?

'You resent my being with child,' she said. 'You're jealous.'

He raised his hand. She saw it, and smiled disdainfully. 'You'd like to hit me, now!'

He saw the disdain and could have killed her. But he continued to remain still, and said: 'I wanted the child . . . if you remember.' His own anger began to melt at the words, and the devil left him. His lip trembled. The tears hurt his eyes. 'This afternoon . . . I thought you might die . . . God knows I've loved you! You ought to remember. . . .'

Linet was convulsed by her own struggle. There was an issue: her devil left her; and suddenly she was in Adrian's arms, crying, 'Oh, I love you! Oh, why do we do this?'

[- 1 8 -]

ONE afternoon the week following Linet came
suddenly to Adrian's room in the tower with horror
on her face. He sprang up. 'Linet! What is it?'

'Adrian! It's Bella! I can't tell you.'

'Bella!' He had thought Linet's time had come,
two months too soon. An instant of relief was
followed instantly by a fresh terror caught from
Linet. Then he stilled himself: there might be
much to be done. 'Is Bella ill? Tell me, darling, if
you can.'

He would hear that Bella had dropped dead, or
was seized with intolerable pain. He moved over
to the telephone, supporting Linet with his arm.

'She's ill. She was so funny. Oh, Adrian, she
must have gone mad!'

'Oh, no!' For Adrian there was nothing more
terrible in the world than madness. 'Why do you
think that? She was suffering bad pain perhaps. . . .'

'She was so funny. She said such strange things.'

'She couldn't bear her pain. What an awful
thing that is! She was just incoherent.' But it was
useless to protest against what he saw in Linet's
eyes. 'What . . . happened?'

'I went in to ask her a question . . . She just sat
there and smiled and said things that were . . .
horrible.'

233

Linet shivered so that Adrian began to fear again for her safety. He put off his thoughts a little by telephoning for the doctor and stopping to settle Linet by the fire. But all at once she controlled herself. 'I mustn't,' she said. 'I mustn't.' Then he stood up. His hands were sweating. 'The doctor can't be here for some time,' he said, forcing his tongue to move. 'I must . . . go and see her.' No, he would not go to Mark in the hope that Mark would go to Bella. He went downstairs and across the hall and along the passage, forcing himself to go unhurriedly, for it would be a sort of cowardice to rush and get it over. But he suffered (especially when he reached her door and stood with his hand on the knob) from faintness. And with one queer disinterested part of himself he noted the worn pattern of the carpet in the passage and a felici-tous arrangement of daffodils in the window beyond. It was without intention, as it were, that he turned the door-handle.

Bella sat idle in her arm-chair, looking out of the window. 'Why shouldn't I rest like other people and enjoy life?' She turned round, and her face wore a look of peculiar gaiety that suddenly changed. She rose to her feet, staring, as if in recognizing Adrian she recognized that some strange thing was happening to her. 'You were always good to me!' she exclaimed. 'You were very kind, when you remembered.' There was an appeal in her voice, and she made as if she would cling to him, she, Bella. He couldn't help it that the contact of her body made him shudder. He overcame that, and said: 'I'll always remember in future. I'll look after you. Nothing shall happen that might make you afraid or lonely.' He spoke to her soul, and her eyes acknowledged his vow. It was the last time on earth that the recognizable Bella was seen.

An hour later, Mark, Linet and Adrian were gathered in the drawing-room for a conference with the doctor. It was a March evening of delicate beauty, with snow in the corners of the terrace and a promise of June in the far parts of the sky. Adrian had not guessed that Mark would feel so badly about Bella's illness, or so frankly shed tears. The doctor explained that a paralysis of the brain had begun: she would die in perhaps twelve months. It would be best to put her in a nursing-home.

Adrian went to the window, wishing he could escape from what he had to say. 'I'm sorry, but I can't allow that. I promised her.'

Linet sat still with her eyes hidden behind one hand. The doctor argued, and his arguments were sound. Adrian felt the others must be bound to agree with him. But they had not heard the promise he made to Bella in the darkening of her mind.

A nurse came; the doctor left: Adrian went over to Linet. 'I'm sorry, my dear. I understand how it will be for you. But there was only one thing to do, I felt. Do you know what I mean?'

'I know you had to do it.' She agreed; but she spoke as if he had, under necessity, done something dreadful.

He knelt by her, and stroked her, longing for a sign. She made one, from the place a great distance off where she was with her child. He felt a pressure of her fingers, saw the flash of a lost Linet in her eyes. Oh, but she will come back in the summer, he thought. I must remember it. 'Naturally,' he said, 'it's bad for you. I understand that it won't make you like the house any better. . . .' There must be no bitterness in his voice. 'I thought I would find you another place, some little house somewhere, in the country perhaps, where you could go till it's over.'

Would she perhaps resent that? He watched her anxiously. But Linet was suddenly there in all her beauty, and a new Madonna-sadness shadowed her face. 'I wouldn't want to be sent away.' They took comfort of each other. Their affection was a candle in a night of disaster.

ADRIAN had made Linet an aviary, an extension
of the greenhouse on a new foundation of concrete,
a swelling glass shape that now wholly filled the
angle between two wings. The semi-circular apartment of moderate temperature that he had con-
trived for the birds, a cage of fine mesh with room
to move round it, occupied the space where the
orchids and poisonous plants had been; those vegetables now flourished in warmth and moisture on the
further side of the glass partition, a green, dripping
universe interposed between that soft and feathery
region and the world beyond it, the world figmented
out of pain. No more such interposition for me,
muttered Adrian while he raked over the sandy
floor of the cage and made a small heap of cabbage
leaves. I'll see God's face . . . but then. . . . A
light that was not light came to him. God is, perhaps, nothing but an interposition; the most
soothing of all pretences between our minds and
. . . what? He straightened himself and wiped
sweat off his face. Of what use to say no more pretence, no more coloured glass, until thought had
conquered the unknown when all his thoughts
turned round with a new face, or rather with no
face? Well, it was always so in the beginning of
great efforts of the mind, according to what one
read.

But who would have thought the world was evil, looking at it in May? Out there, through tints of glass, was a haze of new leaves, laburnum, lilac; one knew that tulips were growing in the garden beds, all the windows of the house were open to let in warm air, and the window boxes were a sight with hyacinths. Everything was as it had been those days when first that fair, graceful Linet came like some being sprung from a narcissus clump into the house. He could have wept at this as at the sudden glimpse of some happiness now inaccessible down vistas of the past. For he could not recover it. He recollected her coming as the dead and damned may revolve old scenes, not quite able to remember how the sunshine felt in their eyes, or why there was ecstasy. Yes, for men all evil the world, evil the life of the senses; and one must leave it behind for a satisfying life of the mind. For these birds, these tiny darting creatures, brown and green and purple and twenty beautiful colours, existence must be nearly all fair, and they could have no concept of sin. He shook his head to think what care men will take of birds, men whose ingenuity has so dismally failed concerning their own affairs; and how they will have a cat in the house to see one conscienceless creature living in ease. And sick cats are quietly put to sleep. But nobody would put Bella to sleep, though not the utmost resources of human knowledge could arrest her paralysis.

Linet would like this when she came home in two or three weeks with the new little caterwauling

Anthony. This world of birds was reality to her: she had not lost Eden. For her the world of pretence was the world where love died. That was the kind of thing she used to pretend to him in the beginning of their commerce, that love always died; to defend her heart from exposure, he supposed, for she had never accepted after all — he was sure of it now — the lessons of her experience, and never would even though Adrian himself should fail. She knew more in her soul than the world could tell her. And as she gained in certainty he gained in confusion, by the very process of taking thought. But Linet too used her intellect and examined herself. She carried self-examination, he sometimes thought, to the point of self-destruction. That must be because she feared nothing in human nature, feared nothing in her own nature, and was ready to lose her life. He saw the excellence of her spirit in that; but it annoyed him sometimes in practice, after they had quarrelled, or nearly quarrelled, that she would show a wish to go over it all again, in order to understand, as she said, the obscure why of their antagonism and haul it out. He explained to himself that he did not want to know her so well, to possess all her secrets; people, especially lovers, should not trespass on each other's personality or invite trespass, he said. There should be courtesy, a sort of formality and distance, between lovers; they should achieve the last revelations of beauty in the formal design of their behaviour. And as to the quarrels between Linet and himself, if they

239

must needs defile the pattern of their life in such a way, he maintained that nothing could be mended by talking. They might always leave everything to the miraculous renewal of their passion. Passion! He hung a bunch of grapes on a branch of the little tree where the birds gathered, and his mind went off on new trains of thought, with hesitations.

The fresh thoughts were not agreeable. In any case, it was fantastic, on an afternoon like this and at such a time to think of their quarrelling. Had he not taken resolutions? Sweet, radiant, plump Linet would come home with Anthony; and they would live in great friendship, at a distance, she occupied with her baby, he with his work, and never dare to darken their happiness with any kind of passion. They would remember Bella's miserable life, and praise God with exemplary conduct for past gifts of heavenly experience. And perhaps, if they lived under this kind of discipline, Adrian would solve problems, achieve perfect means of expression for true beliefs of the creative mind. This sensation of death and withering in his spirit would pass.

He did not grudge Linet her preoccupation with Anthony. It seemed inevitable that for the next few months Adrian must live somewhat on the edge of her interests, and he did not regret it; preferred it, indeed, on account of certain difficult interests of his own. He certainly understood her feelings, for he loved that baby himself. It was reassuring to find himself capable of so much love. He found it difficult to wait until Anthony came home, when he would be able to pick him up without asking a nurse's permission and bring him to this sun-chamber and show him the swarm of birds darting under bright glass. What a pity Bella could never see him! He must never be brought into the presence of her dying mind. Linet would like to sit here, he thought, on summer afternoons, with two or three panes of the glass open, and enjoy her baby and dream her mysterious dreams. How little he knew of her, in spite of her self-exposure; how much less, now. Perhaps the discovered self is the last mystery. Oh dear! Once again his thoughts showed a new aspect. I am really no thinker, he said. The terror took hold of him that his own brain would give way like Bella's. True, he argued, the causes of her paralysis reside in her being female. Or do they? Is there not something analogous in a man that might affect a mind perhaps congenitally unstable! The first few nights after Bella's illness showed itself he had been tortured by that fear, with full return of his old terrors. Who am I, and what is it to exist?

Adrian awaited Linet's return in a state of restlessness. He was hard at work; never, indeed, had his work been so hard; and he would often leave the litter of attempted designs and pace lawn or drive, where he had paced in jealousy so many days after that first Easter, still trying to experience over again the passion that then changed his body into a body of celestial pleasure, to remember the first almost terrible, almost resisted guesses that it was the same with Linet, the anguish of her disappearance, the suffocating doubt and jealousy, the peace that she gave him with her summons to Paris. It had been strange to perceive her sadness in Paris, that sadness of one destined to martyrdom. There was some ineradicable sadness in her nature. She was sad here in this house, and it would be worse now, in spite of the aviary and all he could do to make the house agreeable to her, with Bella so dismally afflicted in that room just out of sight round the corner. He stopped in his walk and considered the rambling, uncoordinated pile, and smiled a little, but sadly. Just as the château stands as the sign of achieved perfection in art and unity of mind, this house is partial, divided and unformed, he said. That is why I cling to it, and Linet, sweet sprite, divine flower, is ill at ease.

When at last Linet returned, that aviary became her sitting-room; she spent the warm, sunny hours there in silence. She seemed tranquil. Never without resource, she cradled Anthony in an orange box and aired his napkins on hot pipes in the orchid-house adjacent. In that mild air she received in succession Mr. Pollock, Tracy, Gwatkin, a congratulatory deputation of three from the factory, and as many Mansfields as could be got in. Adrian was glad to have given her such a place; it seemed unreal, and made their talk harmless. It was removed as far as possible from Bella's room, and Bella coming back from a short walk with her nurse

242

was only a step on the gravel, or perhaps a blurred figure the other side of that screen of glass and plant-forms. The doctor told them that Bella wouldn't be able to walk much longer, and she would disappear into her room. Adrian made a point of seeing her two or three times a day, and suffered abominably from her gay, irresponsible conversation. To spare Linet the onus of a decision he solemnly forbade her from taking any part in the nursing and care of his cousin: she accepted this for the present, and gave herself up to Anthony, and spent her time under glass like a flower.

Adrian continued at work, in furious spasms. Sometimes of an afternoon, smitten with doubt that he was leaving her too long alone, he would go down to the aviary and pick Anthony out of the orange box and direct his remote attention to the flittering birds. Anthony would stare as if profoundly speculating on the nature of existence, or smile suddenly as if he saw something funny in the bright crystalline ceiling; or else he would pucker up his eyes and begin to yell, in which case Linet would seize him and perform those acts that restore peace. And Adrian would discuss him with Linet, and traffic with her in amity, somewhat respectful, somewhat formal. He had never seen her so lovely.

There was an afternoon when Linet emerged a little from her silence. 'What are you so busy at in the tower?' she asked him. He was trying to make Anthony admire two fire finches, but Anthony for the moment preferred to squint at his own bib.

There had been sadness in her voice; it dismayed him.

'Windows for that Theosophical Church.' he said.

'Have you done God yet?'

'Practically.' He had no wish to talk about it, but he owed her the courtesy. 'I've found a sort of formula — I must call it that. It expresses pretty well what I can make out with my thoughts. If they don't understand my designs they can give the job to some other chap.' He said this, perhaps, to Mr. Pollock as well as the gentlemen and ladies who were taking so much interest in the decoration of their place of worship.

'May I see it?'

'Well, I'd rather you waited till it's complete. I'd really rather you didn't see it till I've quite worked it out; or even till the window's in place. There's still a lot to do before I should call the thing finished.' He did not admit to himself why he made these excuses.

She resumed consideration of the birds, in all composure. 'There's a kind of rhythm in their movements,' she said, 'but I can't quite make it out. I wonder why they suddenly fly from one perch to another; or decide in one flight out of scores to peck at a grape, or to have a bath. Is it legitimate to think of them as having enjoyment? Are they happy, would you say?'

'Possibly, in the sense that they're not all at odds and ends within themselves.'

244

She went on watching and asked no more questions. She was terribly attractive; as it were new from some holiday in Paradise and smelling of those fields. If he could take her . . . but he would not.

The weeks slipped by. Tracy, cognisant perhaps of what was going on, perceiving at any rate that Linet and Adrian were out of adjustment, ingenuously cultivated his interests. Sometimes when Adrian approached the greenhouse he would hear Tracy's voice and Linet's laughter. She found Tracy amusing. He accepted the world and human nature, which Adrian never did. 'One must take all opportunities of pleasure,' he said, 'and do no violence to anything in nature.' 'Nature nothing,' Adrian would reply; 'Everything valuable is against nature.' Tracy would lift his eyebrows: 'Valuable! What is valuable but enjoyment?' Linet understood them both. 'Effort is against nature, in love and art,' she observed to Adrian, privately. 'I'm sure the spirit doesn't require the sacrifice of the body or anything human, in a properly balanced person, and isn't any better for it. All sacrifice has to be paid for. You can't healthily give anything up until it no longer interests you.' But Adrian was stubborn, and resisted a sudden demand of his senses for life.

When had it begun, this division of Adrian into parts, mind and matter, flesh and spirit, so that he was not whole in regard to Linet? When had she become an allurement that must be resisted? Why

245

was he now given to thinking of good and evil? He could not bring himself to state it as a situation in which Linet stood on one side and that half-formulated God on the other; for Linet was good, good as anyone in the world, pure in spirit, and his affection for her that made him care for her like a child was good, a golden flower growing from the mud and troubled bottom of his being; and was a man asked to lay all that at the feet of a formula? Adrian meditated in perplexity day after day, week after week. He had lost a secret. If I went to the château now, he said, it wouldn't mean anything to me. I am like a man who has travelled too far from a good place and must go on to a bad one. Often enough, nevertheless, on splendid days in August when Linet was royally serene and beautiful, or on mild, melancholy days in autumn when she sat clouded with sadness, he all but relaxed his grim, ascetic attitude. It was a terrible thing in his nature, and made him afraid, that he would refuse to comfort her lest it should lead to greater softness. He caught sight of his own profile in a photograph one day. That face is arrogant, sensual and cruel, he said. It is imperatively necessary to beat all that down. For a long time he held on his bitter course with an obstinacy that took instructions from some unknown part of him. But common sense made an entrance with somewhat grim and hideous gestures into the struggle between the divided parts of his nature.

On a wet afternoon in November, when the baby

was six months old, Gwatkin brought his long nose to tea. He and Adrian had spent a couple of hours in the tower, going over the books. Gwatkin, now a director of the concern, announced his approval: the output was satisfactory. 'It's an awful bother supervising all that bread-and-butter stuff,' Adrian said. 'D'you know, Gwatkin, I think I shall take a long rest, and let everything run out of my mind and begin new.'

'You can afford a holiday,' Gwatkin said.

They went off in search of Linet. She was in the drawing-room that afternoon, wearing a graceful frock, and Anthony lay in an elaborate cradle, staring with satisfaction into a leafy corner of the ceiling. 'I didn't like to disturb you when you were doing accounts,' Linet said, 'but mother suddenly telephoned to say she'll be coming to tea.'

'Oh!' Adrian was flabbergasted. 'Shall I be in the way?'

'Of course not, darling, I want to exhibit you.' Linet was excited and happy.

Gwatkin shuffled. 'What about me! Perhaps I'd better push off.'

'Certainly not.' Linet put him at ease and showed him what course to take. 'You can both go at the end of an hour, because no doubt mother will want a little while with me alone — if only to apologize for neglect. That was the bell.'

During the few seconds that elapsed before Lady Rockingham was announced, Adrian experienced a decisive mental event. Noticing the way Gwatkin looked at Linet he saw in Gwatkin's face a pre-figuration of what himself might become. If I go on the way I am, he said, I shall be looking at her like that. When the shock of this realization passed, he felt himself relieved of some oppression yet not exhilarated.

One could see at once that Lady Rockingham, dressed in rustling clothes of a past fashion, was Linet's mother. Those were Linet's own features, grown older and more hawklike. Some of Linet's character was present as well — her obstinacy, her directness, and a good deal of her grace. Yes, there was even some hint of Linet's unearthliness: it was possible that this woman and not a fairy gave Linet her soul. The two met and kissed, formally. Adrian was introduced. Gwatkin, and Mark who came in for tea, took to the background, followed from time to time by Lady Rockingham's speculative and, in the case of Mark, startled glances. In fact, she frankly stared at Mark with eyes round and wondering, like Linet's when she watched the birds or a circus. Her coming was opportune. Adrian felt a rising excitement and an anguish. He seemed to fall in love over again with Linet when he saw her in her mother. He felt remorse as well. And all the time he watched the change in himself with a certain mournfulness.

'Your room is remarkable,' Lady Rockingham said. 'Ah, yes, and this is my grandson. The news that one has a grandson is affecting: I had to come sooner or later. My other children do not breed, for some reason. But Linet was always fond of babies, animals and trees.' She fixed her gaze on Adrian. 'Are you fond of children? Did you agree to this, or did she steal it?'

Now Adrian felt quite equal to Linet's mother. 'I hope we shall have nine children,' he replied, with a kind of bitter elation, and looked at Linet, who answered him with an obscure little grimace. Now the memory of first love overcame him, and he had a strange, sad vision of nine elfin children scampering all over the house; sad perhaps because they were nine divided parts of what had been one between him and Linet.

'Nine! It's an ambition,' Lady Rockingham said, 'and one must sacrifice something for an ambition.' Adrian asked himself whether the Mansfields had sacrificed something.

Lady Rockingham went on. 'Anthony, you call him? There are no Anthony's in your father's family, nor in mine. You fancied the name, I suppose. You father will be glad to hear the boy's healthy. No, he won't want to see him. He never cared to see his own children before they were thirteen.'

'Adrian's very good with Anthony,' Linet said.

'Oh yes?' Lady Rockingham gazed at the wall-painting. 'I'm glad to hear it. He will probably look after you.' She flashed at Adrian a glance that he might take for approval. 'Your work, this?'

'Yes.'

'Remarkable; but it makes me feel out-of-doors.

I have never cared for landscape inside houses. One sees enough of it out.'

'You would hardly believe 'mother's drawing-room.' Linet said. 'Windows shut, and a lot of curtains and hangings, and simply thousands of little tables. You haven't changed it, dear?'

'Not in the least, Linet.'

Adrian smiled to hear something acid in the voices of the two women when they made reference thus to their long estrangement. But he was reflecting on what Lady Rockingham had said about his looking after Linet. Did she mean govern her, or care for her? Both, probably. Yes, and like every-one else, she seemed to hint that he had a responsibility.

The old lady beckoned Mark. 'Come here and talk to me. A cousin, I think you said.' She peered closely at her grandson: and Adrian perceived that she was looking for signs of an ugliness that might be in the family. 'You take part in the window-making?'

Mark was serene: 'Yes, I execute parts of Adrian's designs that have to be done with a brush, such as the hands and faces of angels, and now fishes' eyes.'

'I see. Are you married?'

'No. I am not married.' It was wonderful to see the look with which Mark declined any further questions of a personal nature. Good old Mark, Adrian thought. Nevertheless, Adrian was always expecting to observe the signs of Mark's having fallen in love with Linet.

'And Mr. Gwatkin, I think you said?' Evidently Lady Rockingham like to command her surroundings.

'He is our financial controller, our purse,' Adrian explained. 'He opens with difficulty.'

'Very sensible, I'm sure. People can't afford what they used to.' With a few well-directed questions Lady Rockingham found that Gwatkin was connected with friends of that name, and seemed then to dismiss him from her consciousness. Mark and Gwatkin withdrew; and when after a few minutes Adrian proposed to withdraw as well, she detained him.

'D'you find she settles down well?'

'Mother!' Linet broke in, 'you speak of me as if I was a cat.'

'You are, my dear. I always thought of you as a cat.'

Adrian smiled. 'She likes a warm room I've made for her.'

'D'you find her difficult?'

'She's a man's job.' He was quite on fire now.

'Good!' Her ladyship looked pleased. 'I'm sure you'll do it. You look as if you might have good hands with a woman. There's two things needed. One's an imagination few men possess. The other's the back of a hair-brush. The difficulty is to know when to use which.'

Adrian laughed out, because Linet looked so beautifully self-conscious and protesting. 'I shall manage,' he said. 'You can leave her with me.'

251

In the corridor, reflecting on something in his own voice during that exchange, something reassuring and almost noble, he stopped and said to himself: What a prig you are! How you do like to be thought trustworthy and solid! And now you'll have to be!

An hour later, Lady Rockingham desired to be shown over the house. She surveyed Linet's sitting-room, the bedroom, the room that was being planned for Anthony's nursery, the aviary and plant-house, almost without comment. I suppose it all seems very small to her, Adrian thought. She enjoyed the work-room, and it amused Adrian to watch Linet demonstrate to her mother that she could cut glass. As he was seeing Lady Rockingham off they met Tracy coming in. 'Are all these young men Linet's friends or yours?' she enquired.

'If they begin as mine they end as Linet's.'

'Well . . . keep them in order.' Lady Rockingham was driven off in a modest car. It occurred to him that she did not know her own daughter well. And then that perhaps she did.

That night, when Adrian had paid his visit to Bella, he went in search of Linet, somewhat on edge from his contact with the fact of suffering. One must remember, he told himself, it is more likely than not that one will fall into catastrophe. It would have been too much to expect the prolongation of such happiness as we had. Linet was right, perhaps; everything changes, and we should have parted that first night she said so. He remembered how from their bed in the tower they saw the moon, a glowing lotus in the lake of the sky, floating among cloud-islets. He had caressed Linet with a rose and laid it in the valleys of her body; she reclined on a bank of moonlight with closed eyes, or turned her lily-pale face to gaze at him, as if a flower gazed. And she said then, 'We must never accept less.'

She was in her sitting-room, picking dead leaves of salvinia out of the glass tank and prodding a snail with a bodkin. There was something forlorn in her attitude, and it became grievous that he had left her so long, as he now saw, alone. 'Let's go and see what it's like in the orchid-house by night,' he proposed. After all, they might well experience what they had experienced before.

She stood up. 'Have you really come for me?'

'Yes.'

'I'm glad.'

He realized as they made their way to the plant-house with their arms round each other that she had known her isolation. Had she accepted it, or was she making up her mind to a course of action?

'Did you patch it up with your mother?' he asked.

'Yes. She wants us to go there.'

How delicious it was to feel her ribs again under his hand, and the movement of her hip!

They passed through the glass-house of sleeping birds, and found themselves far away in a remote, silent world among plants. They had shut all doors after them, and only a lamp burning at the end of the drive faintly irradiated glass and foliage and flower. At first it was hard to find anything to whisper. It seemed best to take and kiss her, and they clung together, and torrents of rain sluiced the roof. It was warm in there with a faint exciting scent. He found himself slipping through seas of pleasure, deliciously drowning, with Linet's kisses for last consciousness of the world.

'Forgive me,' he whispered at last, 'I left you.' Perhaps she would just accept that. An old queer resentment spoke on the point of extinction.

'It was all strange,' she said. 'We were friends, but we had no contact at all.'

'My work was very exacting,' he put forward. 'But then it always was, though perhaps more than ever now. But I don't offer that as the reason. It wasn't.'

'What was the reason?'

'I'm not sure. I don't know. Let's not explore it.'

'I went away from you when Anthony was coming. Did you get used to my being away, or get to like it?'

'No. Oh, no!' He tried to stop her mouth with kisses, but she would not quite yield until the demands of her spirit were satisfied.

'Have you been jealous of Anthony?'

'Perhaps.' It would do, if she must have a reason. 'As if he meant anything in comparison with you!'

It was marvellous to hold her once more and learn her again. But she suddenly wriggled from his arms, and bent over an orchid. 'You're very

exciting,' she said. 'Or perhaps it's this faint scent.'
She sniffed. 'How sad that one can't enjoy a scent
for more than a few seconds. It seems to get fainter
and fainter and disappear. That's how you feel,
don't you? Yet I suppose the scent's still there,
only noses are weak. It's like that with people:
they can't enjoy one another long, so it often seems.
Have you found that with me?'

'Not the least bit in the world. That's really true,
Linet. You are always more desirable; more than
ever now at this moment.' He felt all the reassurance of passionate desire. How unbelievable his
doubts, his mournfulness now seemed!

'I'm glad you say that,' she replied after a
minute. 'Because I want you.'

I must have been ill, he thought. Starving for
her. He could hardly bear the pressure and exhilara-
tion of this recovered knowledge. The orchids in
their pots now appeared to flicker among the leaves
like tongues of fire. And Linet — was there not all
the marvel of flower-texture in her body ; was she
not herself the white vehicle of some heavenly
passion?

'It will be as it was between us,' she whispered.
'And one day when it seems right I shall want
Selena.'

For the first time he perceived and understood
the disappointement over which she had been so
quiet. It seemed as if she had conceived the picture
of an unearthly child that should be the special
incarnation and sign of their experience.

IT was through Viola Mansfield (now Sinclair)
that Adrian was offered work in Chile. Viola's
husband had been transferred to Santiago, and she
wrote that a Señor Villegas was building some tech-
nical schools and a museum, for which he desired
windows by an acknowledged European artist.
'You ought to come out and inspect site and plans,'
she wrote, 'and go fishing with us in the Andes.
You shall ride mountain-walking horses with a
sheepskin saddle, and learn what a cinch is. I can
see Linet in elegant breeches, pushing through a
jungle of trees and bushes and fording streams.'

He gave Linet the letter. 'It's good of her to
include me,' she said.

In fact Adrian had almost made up his mind to
go alone—sometimes, indeed, he had an almost
violent impulse to do so. He had a very strong
affection for Viola. It would be restful to be with
her, for she was a quiet person and loved him without criticism. Yet what was the use? It would be
restful for the time, but he would only come back
to the same puzzling situation, with no way out of
it save one. They had done their best, since that
reconciliation in the glass-house. Linet had done
hers: he recognized it. He had done his best to live
gracefully, to respect her personality, to respect
his own, to maintain a kind of separateness out of

which they might issue from time to time in love, having the more to give each other the more they reserved themselves. But this attitude of his towards Linet had more the character of policy than feeling; it was a posture, but he was not aware of it. Why? — time and again he revolved the problem as it presented itself to his consciousness — why was it fatal to enter in relations with her? Why did love for ever consume itself in flames?

The curious thing was that disaster so often arose on trivial occasions, as if the daemons that possessed them could only enter by mean doors. They had been happy, after their reunion, for some weeks. Then on a fine afternoon he had left his work to go for a walk with her in Regent's Park, and when they were leaning over the bridge that crosses the lake she suddenly pursed her lips and spat on the back of a duck floating underneath. It seemed to Adrian that people near looked as if they thought her ill-bred, or perhaps mad. He was furious, and said so. A severe, contemptuous look came on her lips. 'People were watching,' he expostulated, seeing with despair that it was already too late. A sense of humour on either side would have saved them, but neither could manage it.

'Do you think I mind what people think of me?' she asked.

'Possibly not, but I do.' But already she had made him feel like a fool.

'If you wanted a conventional, doll-like, obedient woman you should have married someone else.'

'I am conventional. I don't need not to be.'

'Yes, and you'd like to kill all spontaneity in me. You think like any bourgeois.'

This hit him where it hurt badly, even though he knew that she couldn't mean it. They went home separately. It took about fifteen minutes for his anger to run off, and three days to win her back. Then there was contrition and passionate amendment.

They strove against this disease of the soul with all their might, but the animosity that made so little into so much seemed to have its own life. Malignant daemons had established a place in their constitutions, and seemed determined to eject all else. Yet, whenever they were on the point of separation, the daemons retired, as if life and enjoyment for the daemons depended on their being kept together. The the daemons returned, usually when Linet and Adrian had begun to congratulate themselves; and Adrian, brooding in his tower, would say to the roofs opposite, I am sick of this idiotic, recurring pattern. Their quarrels had a regular growth, flowering and death. Adrian was convinced that more often than not, perhaps always, it was he that brought it about; but he could not usually tell how or why. He did not excuse himself even if it was she who when the thing had begun could not escape from her mood. He would offend her, often without knowing it until her face told him, drive her away, put out the light in her; sometimes, by a prodigious effort of nerves and brain, he found means to soften her quickly; but as a rule, especially when exhausted by creative effort, he lacked patience, and certain results would follow in an invariable and dreaded sequence. After a long silence and weariness for which he could not help seeming to reprove her, she would enunciate a cynical philosophy that he thought hideous and said so. She would then analyse his motives with a logic that nothing escaped but the truth, as he saw it; and if he replied that she destroyed his own picture of himself as her lover and the person she depicted could no longer presume to offend her with his society, she would accuse herself of something more black than murder and weep like the damned. And Adrian would grow hysterical, without the cruelty to beat her or the skill to cure her with comfort. It was a question of waiting, or wrestling with her, or submitting to a painful analysis, until her mood had eaten itself up and changed naturally into contrition, and they would take one another for pure grief. Then indeed would follow a time when they loved with a mutual and unhindered passion from which all hate and contempt had been purged; but the experience was too harrowing, too degrading, and both lived in dread of it with remorseful memories. It would be better to separate than to tear each other with a blind cruelty that used for its obscure purposes the ancient power of their love.

Bella's death shocked them out of themselves for a time, and sadly brought relief from the conflict of their personalities. After being unconscious and helpless for several weeks, Bella died in March, two months before Anthony's second birthday, on a Wednesday at midnight. During those last hours she made a kind of sighing that filled the house. Mark and Linet and Adrian listened in horrified silence: the doctor had told them she was going. It was in accordance with some ancient piety that Mark and Adrian, and Linet because she was Adrian's wife, went when they were sent for to watch while the changed figure in the bed died in loneliness, without a sign that she knew of friends standing by.

A silence fell on the house, and strange peace. It was a recognizable Bella once more whose head pressed deep into the smoothed pillow: they recovered her in her death. Adrian filled her room with funeral flowers, heavily scented. It seemed strange that she must leave that room and go out of the house, now she was so contained, so much herself. But on the third day there was a hearse in the drive, and her flower-loaded coffin was carried to it past the holly trees, along the terrace and across the lawn, and Adrian drove after her with Mark in a carriage, Mr. Mansfield and the Reverend Eugene Pollock following in another, and critically listened to the funeral words, and returned, and gave orders that her room, still heavy with the scent of lilies, was to be closed.

Afterwards they all talked in the allusive and reminiscent way that people do after funerals.

'You cannot but be relieved,' Mr. Mansfield said; 'it must have been very painful.'

'Yes, we are relieved.' Adrian reflected. 'There is a little less pain in the world; unless pain is a constant, and Bella's portion has now passed to someone else. We shall be able to forget pain sometimes now. But perhaps that's not possible; perhaps one ought not to. Perhaps we should daily remind ourselves that people suffer, that there is little else but suffering, squalor and ugliness of mind. We are not entitled to forget, perhaps, until we have suffered everything in our own body. Do you suppose if anybody took the whole pain and ugliness of life into his own mind and body for a moment the world would have a momentary experience of relief?'

No one answered his thoughts except Linet, who said: 'I used to think joy was a state that we could attain permanently by studying. But it seems as if we have to pay our part of some debt.'

She and Adrian exchanged looks, and Mr. Mansfield observed them. 'It is attainable,' Adrian asserted; 'but only by the most difficult of techniques, and perhaps only after æons of existences. It is simply unity of mind, the disappearance of inferior preoccupations, the union of life and consciousness within the creature so that there forms within him a new person . . .' But Adrian suddenly stopped, knowing that what he said must be obscure to them; and he was inhibited, as usual, by the fear of giving himself away.

'We ourselves had pleasant news,' Mrs. Mansfield said: 'the very day you told us of Bella's death. May I tell you? Andrew and Marigold are engaged, both of them to young people we like.'

Adrian and Linet offered congratulations. Adrian thought of the full measure of happiness that the Mansfields enjoyed. 'Happiness lies in the character,' he said. 'One feels that what people suffer they make for themselves in some way, and can unmake. For me, that is a not intolerable answer to the problem of pain. But I don't really know if it'll do. . . .'

Mr. Mansfield and Adrian were left alone for a few minutes. 'Linet is not looking well,' Mr. Mansfield said.

'No, she is not.' Adrian prepared to defend himself.

Mr. Mansfield omitted a number of steps in the progress of his thoughts. 'Linet is in a manner of speaking frail,' he said. 'I mean in this sense, that she is not a moral being except by her own light. And if that light were put out, if what she believed in failed her. . . .'

'I am not sure that I agree with you,' Adrian replied. 'You mean she might easily go to pieces!'

'Precisely.'

Adrian kept silence, declining further conversation on this subject. Rather impertinent of Mansfield, he thought, when the visitors had gone. But he felt subdued and unresentful, inclined to resignation. The scent of funeral lilies was still in the air.

It was in this mood that they went to the unveiling of Adrian's theosophical windows, an event attended by a crowd at once fashionable and eccentric, including many Americans. Adrian had been unwilling to go, more unwilling to take Linet; and he had nothing but contempt for the refined criticism he heard in the neighbourhood, nothing but hatred for his windows. He felt a certain amusement too: that main window, that startling geometry, that rhythm intended to be God, was after all nothing more than a spider's web with a nucleus in the middle of it (or rather somewhat brilliantly out of the middle). He felt inclined to point this out to the critics who exclaimed over his originality, his daring, his masterly exploitation of clear glass, his sweeping rhythm (there was a lot about rhythm), his profound meaning. He laughed over that especially: there was everything in the windows but meaning. Best thing to laugh. He witnessed the end of his creative life in a mood of ironical resignation. Linet, sweet darling, said not a word; but he knew that her unerring judgment agreed with his. It became necessary to stifle his thoughts in case for some strange reason he should turn and wreak everything on Linet. When they left the building, the God in the window seemed to hold up a pattern of hands; and it felt to Adrian as if, expelled from Eden, he looked back and saw neither flaming brand, nor dreadful faces, nor fiery arms, and dropped no natural tears.

It had been Adrian's proposal that this year they should go away by themselves, with Anthony, instead of visiting the Mansfields as every year hitherto. Linet had perturbed him by her hesitation. She only agreed with reluctance, as if she feared they were not capable of being alone together. But alone they were, up in the mountains with glimpses and wide views down valleys crammed with olive and vineyard and sweet chestnut to stretches of the sea. It was a dreadful journey, because Anthony was awake and energetic all through the night, although his resourceful mother, impervious to the glances and fidgeting of strangers, provided a cradle which she swung from rack to rack. He sobered at his first daybreak view of mountain village and torrent on the Italian side, and gave them an hour of silence; but the broiling, pitiless afternoon from Turin to Genoa was too much for him, and when they got out at Rapallo they were both too hot and exhausted to enjoy the caress of Italian air and strong Mediterranean smell. And now that it was no longer convenient, Anthony fell asleep. The rest of their journey was strange and exciting. They were driven through the streets of Rapallo to a place where the road ended on the wooded flanks of a mountain. Mules awaited them, in charge of a peasant. The luggage was strapped on; they mounted, and Adrian took his sleeping son in his arms; the attendant made an observation of some kind to his animals and they began to climb a winding, stony path. At first they met signs of human existence — the gate of a villa with lantern flickering in ivy at the bend of steep stairs, an inn with ghostly inhabitants murmuring at the door, a light burning before a flower-decked Madonna in some wayside chapel. But the path climbed the ridge of their mountain in steep zigzags, and presently the lights of Rapallo were far below, and the mules went clicking upwards in darkness, under heavy trees. Adrian could see that Linet was transported, away from her mule, deep in black shadows among sweet chestnuts in the valley, high up the opposite mountain-side under pines, far off on that wooded hummock whose golden shoulder told them the moon was rising, adrift on that shining gleam of the sea. They came out soon on a little grassy plateau thick with great daisies, and rested. The valley below them opened towards the Mediterranean. The disc of the moon rose over an edge of forest; profiles of wooded mountain broke the mysterious sea with a faint presence of moonshiny foam; the lights of Rapallo, and tiny harbours in the huge and mountain-broken sweep of the bay, paled. Adrian watched Linet, silent and straight in her saddle. The child in his arms stirred and uttered a little cry.

Yes, it was too mysterious to speak. Mysteriousness floated down like a cloak from the height where they were going and hid them from one another. Anthony slept again, and the mules' feet clicked on the stones. Sometimes they went steadily upwards on paths under tunnels of trees, sometimes steeply on open hill-side with a tumult of faint mountain tops opening to view as they came higher. A beacon suddenly shone out among the trees on the ridge ahead. 'That's it,' Adrian whispered, and now Linet urged her mule to his side to answer: 'There cannot be wickedness here.'

They fell silent to stare at the place they were coming to. The path led them under the wall of a monastery and between huge gateposts. Here the ridge flattened out and broadened into an avenue. On their right hand was the whitewashed and gleaming inn where they were to stay; ahead of them, a sweep of steps in three terraces, wide, shallow and harmonious, led to the doors of a Moorish-looking church and group of ecclesiastical buildings: there was nothing on this mountain but the inn, the monastery and the church.

Adrian stared about him. 'We've left the world,' he said. 'This is like Heaven. We shall see angels going in and out of those doors. There are some at the door of the inn.'

But the two beings seated at a rustic table were secular visitors enjoying a bottle of Orvieto. They looked on in a polite way while the new-comers dismounted, and made a few comments in German. Anthony woke, and was carried bawling upstairs and along echoing corridors to the bedroom. The

266

room was bare; there was a crucifix on the wall;
they put their heads out of the window and looked
straight down a rocky pitch into the shadows of a
deep hollow in the mountains. Out and away from
them, woods fringed the hollow in a grand curve,
entangling the stars. Linet soothed Anthony and
showed him the view; and the lovers, for that they
were in this mysterious moment, stood by the window with their child between them and gave one
another kisses. But Anthony tried to obtain Adrian's
share.

The life they began next morning was idyllic with
a dash of the earthly provided by Anthony, who
usually, when they were in love with mountain,
sea and sun, immersed himself in a squalid pre-
occupation with dirt-pies, or intruded the demands
of nature on their entranced silences. It was a
time of pause. The inn itself became an object of
their affection. Bare, clean and trim, it was intended
to be a hostel for pilgrims. There were no pilgrims
just now, save those worldly ones who toiled up the
mountain from Rapallo in order to sweat, and there
was a delicious sunny quietness in the long corridors.
Besides Adrian and Linet the only visitors were the
German and his girl, who spent their days in the
practice of sun-worship and natural mysteries.
They were large and fair, and one might catch a
brown glimpse of them in the woods. Pleasant-
spoken people they were, of serious intelligence and
great eaters; it was nice to have their company of
an evening at supper with two or three priests in

the refectory, where the innkeeper kept a stock of picture-postcards, necklaces made out of nuts, and holy talismans. Linet and Adrian were not there much during the day. They would take their mules and ride, sometimes into the tumult of mountain-tops, sometimes by a path through the woods and across country to a place where they could go down the steep hillside by sharp zigzags to the sea. Adrian dreamed, not without sadness, not without misgiving, over the sight of Linet, so golden with sunlight, so profoundly thoughtful, so elegant astride her mule in lilac shirt and green shorts, riding like a fairy. He would hold Anthony in front of him on the mule's neck, or walk and let the child ride in the saddle, holding his hand; and they would go clicking and slipping down to the cove, in great pleasure of the enterprise. It was a tiny cove between mountain-sides, with nothing but a few cottages, a monastery now inhabited by fisher-men and their multitudinous children, and a place where you could buy wine and drink it under vine-leaves in an arbour. Every morning at eleven o'clock a little steamer came in from Rapallo, sometimes bringing people who wished to make a picnic. In that case Linet and Adrian would take their boat and row out to sea until they seemed alone in a sun-drenched, undulating immensity. But usually they had the cove to themselves, and once the natives were used to them, they played unregarded. Their skins turned a rich brown. Anthony spoilt one of Linet's dreams. In her visions of the holiday she had seen him swimming, a naked brown baby in blue sea. He was willing to be naked, but he refused boisterously to enter the sea. It was thus necessary that one of them should take charge of him while the other went swimming in the deep, transparent water, or nosing alongside the rocks. Sometimes Linet would float face downwards almost a half-minute, watching the swarms of fish that darted underneath her, peering into that world of queer forms, blue luminous depths and sea-green light, amber-shot; sometimes she would climb out on to a pulpit of rock and dive and dive until, because her head sang, she was willing to obey the protests that Adrian, with Anthony tucked under one arm, shouted to her from the rocks. Then they would eat their lunch under the vine-leaves and drink wine; and they would clamber out along the rocks until they found some place where they could put Anthony to sleep in shadow; and they would lie down, and turn to one another. Often on those long splendid afternoons she slept, soothed into sleep by the warm-fingered sun and the whispering Mediterranean; and while she lay beside him so still Adrian would look into her face for signs of what her soul thought.

For as the days went on Adrian could not hide from himself that he was subject to sadness and stranger moods. He hoped Linet did not know it, but he couldn't be sure. What unknown passion was it that so violently reinforced moods of sadness,

269

self-criticism and despair; what floating anger that attached itself to his thoughts, so that all of a sudden, in some moment of peace, he would be arguing hotly with the image of Linet, anticipating her answers with a kind of scorn and scorifying her? He tried his best to free his spirit from that body of emotion; but when most conquered it seemed most lively, and most strongly existed when he thought it dead. There was always an hour or two in the early evening, when Linet was putting Anthony to bed, that he had to himself. He enjoyed this liberty and dreaded it at the same time; for it was then that moods were apt to possess him. In old days, sitting in front of the Inn with a glass of wine, he would have been taken with a desire for prolonged solitude, for weeks alone with Linet in this beautiful scenery, when he would compose the long enjoyments of his senses in glass, or in some new medium. That was not happening now. He was not creative. Worse, sometimes he was not alive to his surroundings. Pine-tree, vine-yard and terra-cotta farmhouse on the hill-side had lost meaning: he recognized it, and looked round in a panic to see if there was any significance left for him in green stretch under chestnuts or vermilion tumult of mountain-tops over there beyond the church and the trees. Oh yes, and that last great window was a sign of death in his spirit. . . . But then Linet would come to the door in her pretty apron; and at the sight of her, so fresh, so mysterious, like some figure of the moon risen over a meadow, he would wonder at his own thoughts. He had not yet quite lost Linet's meaning, anyway; or the skill to dispel the sadness that hovered in her face when she saw the departing sunset glow of his mind.

If he could know why the window that everyone praised for its intricate and mathematical austerity was a failure, it might be possible to amend this dryness of the whole nature in which the world lost value and reality, a dryness liable to be drowned with unexplained, undue emotion. Sometimes he longed for an escape from everything that might provoke these distempers. 'I ought to have been a monk,' he would say, brooding under the wall of the monastery; and he said it to Linet once in the refectory when they had with them at dinner an ecclesiastical dignitary. 'I think I should have done well in the Church.'

'You certainly have the face for it,' she replied. 'Women would love you.'

'I had been thinking of myself as rather withdrawn from women,' he said. 'Rather thin and pale and ascetic.'

'Ascetic nothing!' She laughed at him. 'You won't be ascetic till you're dead, except by violence. You were born to be a woman's lover.'

He grinned. 'Oh well! I'll be a worldly prelate and wear scarlet!' But he was a little reversed.

He pondered these thoughts in the church one evening. Born to be a woman's lover — dark destiny for the clear spirit in man! All at once he seemed to feel the essential nature of women as a force of great sweetness and danger, like the darkness and incense of this church. There was almost no light in the church save a little radiance around three tiers of candles before an image, for the windows were small and remote and cob-webby. It was possible to descry the sacred picture above the high altar, and a fern-decorated fountain from which they drew curative waters. Perhaps I shall take a draught, Adrian said. There were gleams of gilt and strong colours in the vault of the ceiling, and everywhere the shimmer of silver from hundreds of little votive offerings, hearts, limbs and diminutive likenesses of those who had received grace and healing. I'll dedicate a silver heart, Adrian said, if on this sweet mountain I am delivered from apprehension, anger and pride; if I achieve love without hate. If Linet could hear my prayer, she could understand perhaps that my will is to love her. At once a trace of animosity appeared in his feelings: had not Linet also some need of deliver-ance from the worse part of herself? He saw dark thoughts coming up like clouds charged with storm. Yes, for certain he was in a kind of sympathy with women and churches; the twilight in them, perhaps. He had a sudden curious access of regret for a lost self that once made windows of great richness and splendour, expressing itself in a tumult of ruby, purple, and green. Now that self dealt in abstrac-tions, and the rejected colours took their revenge in the shapes of angers and despairs. He held this thought a moment, and lost it in a crowd of thoughts following, a complex of which established themselves when he said: I hate women, for they cloud the clear part of me with emotions; and, there is something in me that is deeply offensive to women and makes grief. But there was Linet standing beside him in the twilight. He took the hand that she pushed into his and felt remorse.

The air was wonderfully fresh outside. They ran all down the steps hand in hand, and raced in the avenue, much to the amusement of an aged priest and scandal of a young one. It was exhilarating. Adrian, sounding himself, was happy to find himself exhilarated. They watched the deep colours fade from the tops of the mountains, and dined by themselves at a wooden table in front of the Inn. It was a deep, a holy night. An odour of pines and fig trees came from the mountains. They drank yellow wine. All Adrian's genius for Linet woke, and when the church clock rang midnight she was in his arms, spell-bound.

The next morning they were about early, for the magnificent serenity of the sky and their own happiness seemed to call for a prolonged sojourn in the cove. This morning, Adrian wondered at his doubts of the day before; the wooded mountain-shoulders, the glittering sea, the cottages and odorous farms, the scent of olive and fig, the peasants soft-stepping and balancing like animals, the tufts of grass and very stones of the steep path, the heat itself, had all beauty and meaning. And

Linet, was she not radiant! He admired her as she rode; loved her fine shoulders and the proud breasts that declared themselves in her lilac shirt, the firm shapely buttocks that answered the movements of her saddle; loved her mysterious, sweet face.

'Well, Anthony,' he said, hugging the child in front of him. 'You've got a lovely mother.'

'Smim, smim,' said Anthony, meaning that to-day he would go in the water and swim. He meant it always on the way down, but actual contact with that odorous, strange Mediterranean terrified him. Adrian understood, for he himself in some moments had a certain terror, especially at night, of that whispering, haunted sea, and indeed of the mountains themselves, full, as he felt them, of old gods and daemons. Once this morning, swimming under the rocky cliffs in that magical water, he turned suddenly for the beach where Linet sat small and bright with Anthony crawling over her knees; he was terrified that the living rock would stretch out a hand, or some strange being draw him down to the kingdom under the sea. Linet had the same terror, he knew; but she braved it out. While she was swimming he lay and stared at the mountains. How still it was up there in the hanging woods; how fresh the pine-trees, how brilliant the rocks! Up there in the mornings daemons slept, invisible; in the afternoon and the evening they would be all about the path and among the bushes, an invisible movement, ready to enter the souls of men. He

274

looked out to sea, and there was Linet's small head, lifting and sinking with the rise and subsidence of a swell; he almost shouted to warn her against things that might draw her under. But she came back safe, and they took their lunch under the vine-leaves, and lay down in the shade, and swam again; and the sun declined a little, and it was time they took Anthony home. 'Thank God for the mules,' Adrian said, looking up at the heights. 'Suppose we had to climb up there on our feet.'

'I did think of making Anthony a little sack and having him on my back,' Linet said.

'You would think of something rather charming and slightly impracticable.'

'Oh, you think you're practical, do you?'

'Very!'

'That must be nice for you!'

He grinned. 'Off you go. Mount!'

She mounted, in a businesslike manner. 'How white your teeth are!' she said. 'They look nice in your mahogany block.'

He reached up and drew her head down to kiss her.

It was perhaps the most magnificent afternoon they had seen. Many times they drew rein at some turn of the path, and sat there staring to right and left at unfolding vistas. The mountains opened; the horizon of the sea widened into misty immensities, the pine trees burned. When they reached the top Adrian dismounted and, put Anthony in the saddle. How peaceful it was, and heavenly, to walk homeward in all that splendour of mountain, forest and sky, holding Anthony by the hand, listening to his puny bullying of the mule. He could watch Linet too, sweet patch of lilac and green riding ahead of him. And he could see, when she drew rein and waited for them to come up, that her spirit was far away. He was contented and, when at last they reached home, very tired.

They dined out of doors in the last warmth of the sunset. Adrian enjoyed his dinner; Linet was silent; night fell. About half-past ten, when Anthony had been seen to, Linet proposed that they should go for a little walk. 'A little one, then,' Adrian agreed. They walked arm-in-arm along the avenue, up the broad steps, and round behind the church and its buildings. They found themselves in a rambling flagged passage between houses with barred windows. 'Probably was a nunnery once,' Adrian said. 'They look dark and empty now.' He enjoyed the romantic passage, the fine proportions of the houses, and there through that opening a great and dreamy stillness of trees; he was at peace.

'I wonder what it's like in a nunnery,' Linet said.

'No idea. Let's sit down on this window-sill and just stare at the woods.'

'Like cows in a field at night.' There was no irony in her voice; her voice was empty. Adrian scanned her face, and saw she was engaged with her thoughts.

They were silent until she said: 'It might be a

good life for a woman. I mean if you cut out the sublimated sex, the ecstatic part of it, and gave yourself up to work of some kind.'

'It might, yes.' Adrian assented, out of politeness; but her words awoke no answering ideas in his drowsy mind.

'Do you think,' Linet asked presently, 'that perhaps one ought not to bring a woman into the world?'

'Well, really, I don't know.'

'Surely you've got some ideas on the subject?'

'I suppose I have. But not when I'm sleepy.'

'Well, it's rather important, I should have thought.'

He was puzzled by something in her voice, and took her hand to show that he was friendly disposed. She let her hand lie there.

'I mean,' she said, 'that we've thought about having a girl; and it's reasonable to discuss whether we ought to.'

To Adrian it seemed quite the wrong moment. 'I agree,' he replied. 'But at some time when it is spontaneous with both of us to do so.'

'That was the time to be spontaneous,' she replied. 'Won't you ever talk with me about anything important?'

Adrian's mind woke into full activity. He saw in a flash that she had wished to complete the marvellous experience of this day with the begetting of a daughter, who should presently be in the world as the sign of their nights and days here, with all

277

the magic of mountains, forest and sea in her body. He took her shoulders urgently. 'Of course I'll talk now. Yes, I think it right, necessary, that you should bring another woman into the world.'

Her body did not yield. 'Men only think about food and sleep, I suppose.' He understood with a horrible sinking of the heart that he responded too late. There was a rush of resentment, too; why could she not make some little allowance for his natural fatigue? And at the same time he recognized that her own spirit burned bright and indefatigably.

'You will never discuss anything with me,' she said.

'I will discuss anything you like.' He urged it.

She turned her face away from him and spoke to the dreaming trees. 'Men do not know what love is,' she began.

He interrupted: 'They do. They know more than women!' But he felt pitiably mortal. 'Is there no relenting in angelic natures?' he asked.

'Men are blind and mad and damnable,' she went on. 'They destroy what is most beautiful in life because of their awful pride. They cannot be humble and give themselves. They must be sacred and untouchable, and a woman may die of anguish but they won't open their hearts. I know it. Oh, but I was a fool when I knew it all along. Everything changes, nothing remains the same, and love especially disappears. A man's love, that is. A woman, poor beast, can't stop.'

Now Adrian knew that he was possessed by a deadly anger. 'Do you forget everything for so little?' he asked.

'For so little!' She smiled with an infuriating contempt.

'Linet! No man has ever loved a woman as I have loved you. . . .'

'Oh, I daresay. As a man may. I don't deny that I've pleased you greatly in bed. . . .'

He seized her by the neck and let go again. In a minute, if she looked at him with so much contempt, he would have to kill her or else run, run down the mountain and into Rapallo and into the sea. He controlled his hysteria. 'That's a pretty bad thing to say.'

'Whenever have you given yourself to me? Oh you don't know, Adrian, how distant and utterly cruel you are!'

'Cruel? I don't understand. I simply don't understand!' He looked from side to side, at the barred windows and glittering night, and wondered if madness had fallen on him.

'Yes, men are simply wrapped up in themselves,' she said. 'Oh, I admire it! I should be the same if I were a man. I should take my pleasure of many women, and waste no pity on them — I understand them too well. I despise them. I despise myself. I should have held by what I knew, and never given myself over to any man to stay with me out of pity.'

'But this is simple nonsense,' Adrian said, getting colder the more he yielded himself to fury, while a part of him stood aside as it were and pointed out the truth, namely that he had profoundly failed with her.

'Why not face the facts?' she asked. 'I please you as a mistress, except that I'm not doll-like and obedient enough, and you hate it when I want to talk about important things. For you don't love me. I have no part in your thoughts. You don't tell me what you're thinking and imagining. . . .'

'How the hell can a man!' he burst out. 'This is simple nonsense!'

'Yes, my thoughts are simple nonsense! What I think and imagine and want is simple nonsense!'

'These are not your thoughts. It is not Linet that thinks and talks that way. Linet isn't here, but some other thing. Linet has lost her meaning.' He suddenly felt that with appalling force. No meaning in Linet. No significance in love. The world dropped away under him. 'God! that we should be talking like this, in this place. Let's stop quickly, Linet, please!'

Yes, it was queer to see two beings in human form watching each other with so much animosity, in that passage on a summer night, saying such bitter things.

'Human beings cannot know and understand one another,' she began.

'Wait,' he said. 'Let's stop. Let's remember yesterday and to-day. Please Linet! Can't you just recall for a moment how happy we were, and come in my arms?'

'How happy you were? Was I happy? Did I not know there was some reason for unhappiness?'

'I shouldn't say things like that,' he urged. 'Darling, relent a little. Kiss me.'

'One is absolutely alone in this world,' she said. 'One must recognize it. Love and all my thoughts about it are just illusion.'

'Kiss me!' he urged. 'In a minute it may be too late.'

But she was a stone. 'One can't amend things like that.'

Now he was taken with too much anger. Once more he seized her neck and began to press his thumbs into her throat. He didn't know what it was that made him relax. Her face changed most miserably. 'Oh!' she wailed. 'Oh!' and with that cry she ran from him.

PART III

[- 1 -]

WHEN he came to her beautiful house in the Avenida Vicuña Mackenna, Viola made no secret to·Adrian of her pleasure in his arrival. The sight of her should have opened wounds and touched fountains; but emotion was all run out, and there was no other event in him than the springing up of a little green feeling like a plant in a barren place. He did not need the self-assurance that her recognition produced, for in those melancholy Argentine plains, in remote dusty towns where accordion-music blaring from corners outwent sadness, in the nipping passage of the Andes, in the extreme of what was unfamiliar, his personality had held. Fear with regret and anger, had retired out of exhaustion. Yes, Adrian had hated Linet for a time; but now hate and all passion had run down to nothing, and it was simply true that he loved Linet no more. This was great loneliness. He held Viola's hand and grimly meditated.

'How brown and weatherbeaten you are!' she exclaimed. 'You came alone?'

'Yes.'

Viola listened intently to echoes of what she heard in his voice. Then grief came into her eyes, grief for many things, he divined.

283

'May I ask questions?'
'No.'
'Is that fair, Adrian?' She meditated and found nothing to say, except: 'You've come here to plan windows?'

'I shall never make another!' He laughed. 'You should see my last one. A portrait of God in a theosophical church. A beautiful geometry. A portrait that Adam might have made out of his memories after he lost Eden. I'm no longer even old Adam; too drained. But I'm talking too much . . . it's nice to see you.'

He looked into her lovely modest eyes and she looked back. 'You always had a strong dose of old Adam,' she said. 'It wouldn't be you without him. Poor Adrian, you do look weather-beaten.' Her eyes filled with tears. 'I must ask . . . I don't see what to do unless I know . . . Have you two . . . parted?'

He nodded, and she went very white. 'It's a little late for me . . . Oh! I think of myself when I should think of you and . . . her!'

Adrian refused to be affected by any picture of Linet in grief. 'I'm cut off from all my sources,' he said. 'I start in the world new.' He wouldn't let her talk any more about anything past. 'This is a new world anyway. There is complete separation from that old one up there on the other half of the globe. People must do their best there for themselves. It's many weeks ago, that old one. Isn't your name Sinclair? Really, Viola, I find it quite

284

impossible to recover any feeling of what life was like before I arrived this side the Andes. How stupendous they are! Once that height would have terrified me!' He looked out of her window, and across her garden where humming birds hung whirring against the flowers, and saw white peaks high in heaven. 'What weather! Is it always like this?'

'Not always like this. But for months at a time like a hot and perfect June day in England.'

'Where's England?'

She accepted his attitude, perforce. 'Of course you'll stay here,' she urged.

'No I won't. I'll stay at the Crillon, even if they do clean everything with petrol. I have a luxurious suite there with crimson curtains and a pink carpet and a fine bathroom with silver fittings. It's very spacious. I have plenty of room.'

'Well, you'll come to dinner to-night?' Viola displayed an eagerness that seemed oblivious of all but the moment. 'We dine at half-past nine here; but do come before that, for cocktails.'

Adrian found Viola's husband, Walter Sinclair, head of the Chilean branch of a great merchant firm, rather difficult to talk to. He was interesting, intelligent, affable; more than that, one could see that a woman might be fond of him; but a slight uncomfortable tension established itself between him and Adrian. My fault, Adrian reflected. I dare say he's not conscious of it. On my side it's because I've seen that Viola's on edge with him.

They sat at dinner in a fine dusky room with windows opening on a garden. 'You're just travelling?' Sinclair enquired. 'Viola has spoken of you. I've never had the opportunity to see one of your windows. As a matter of fact, I'm never comfortable in a church.'

'My windows aren't all in churches.' But Adrian didn't want to talk to the man about windows; and in any case the man obviously had no feeling for any form of art: for him, it was just something pretty that you buy. And in any case, Adrian reflected, you have ceased to create; the being that made use of you has withdrawn his patronage.

It was perhaps the challenge of Viola's presence that prevented an uprising of grief. He watched her perfect comeliness, tasted her repose that was a little ruffled now by his own arrival. Yes, she would be a quiet person to live with; she would enjoy complete happiness and tranquillity with the man that she loved. Viola became the sole object of his attention. She pinned him to the spot; kept him from going back over the Andes. Useless, further to revolve that insoluble, maddening problem of Linet and Adrian, Adrian and Linet. A little drained recollection died easily among the lava-remains of his emotions. Here the only green thing and refreshed part of him was this affection for Viola.

After dinner they sat in the garden. It was very still. A lawn stretched before them between banks of some unrecognized flower; on either hand stood

286

a row of fruit-trees; there, beyond the glimmering roof of a neighbour's villa, were clouds rolling in the moonlight and stupendous shapes.

Adrian was fascinated by his own feelings. A detached, a skilled man could live a different life every week, with different people. There was a special friendship between Viola and himself that demanded life and fulfilment. Something was due to it. Adrian remembered once asking himself how would Viola conduct herself if he tempted her. It had become a question of importance.

The Sinclairs certainly gave him a wonderful time. They introduced him widely. He was invited to many houses and for week-ends at country farms. The Sinclairs, most popular, but whether for both their sakes or for hers alone was not certain, were usually there; but though there was no lack of musky nights in Chilean gardens Viola and Adrian were almost never alone, except in the morning if perhaps he met her out shopping, or in the hot afternoons if she asked him to tea. These occasions became precious. They grew to be conscious of the separation imposed on them in society; they would glance at one another in a garden at night. Yet Adrian was slow to put the thing in decisive action. Undoubtedly by now he would have liked to take Viola and kiss her, if only for a kind of salvation in passionate contact. But he refrained; partly because the sources of action were ice-bound; partly, perhaps, because of an old humility, natural with him: he was not sure, in spite of clear evidence, that she desired it, or even that she was better than just friendly disposed.

They found it curiously difficult to make conversation. There was embarrassment when their eyes met. Sometimes he would offer to read from some book he wished her to appreciate, and she would accept with a soft 'Please'. He derived pleasure from it if any passage delighted her.

'Did you really enjoy that?' he asked her one afternoon.

'Yes. It gave me very pure satifaction.'

Something in her voice surprised him. Did she intend sarcasm? He rose and put the book back in its case. Through a wide-open window he could see humming-birds whirring over the flowers in the garden. No, he decided; if I take her kisses now, that will bring an ending of some sort. An ending would only begin new difficulties. He said: 'I don't think I shall read to you again.'

'Why?' she innocently asked.

'I don't really know. To-morrow you shall take me to the cemetery instead. I like foreign cemeteries. They are very expressive.'

'To-morrow is Saturday. You're coming to the farm with us for the week-end.'

'So I am. How happy that will be!'

They smiled at each other, and an uncomfortable significance lapsed from their conversation.

[- 2 -]

NEXT morning they drove away to St. José de Maipu — the Sinclairs, Adrian and a Captain and Mrs. Ross in one car, with four others in a second: Sinclair liked his week-ends well populated. The road ran alongside the Andes, that seemed only a few fields away. Adrian sat between the two women. He couldn't talk for watching the mountains, waiting at every turn for some new white presence in the sky, some fresh stupendous confection of rock and snow. Sometimes the roof of the car cut off his view and he leaned over to get a glimpse. It was pleasant, then, to have Viola's face so close; to know that she was sharing a certain solemnity that he felt in presence of that terrific scenery.

The road turned in towards the range, and the high peaks disappeared behind nearer masses of rock. They passed miles of forest and green seas of scrub, ever mounting until the gentle wooded hills gave way to wilder contours with snow traces not far above the road. They swung and jolted over ruts and potholes, crossed and recrossed a single-track railway that looped like a switchback, crept along a ledge with rock overhead and a torrent below, deep among mountains. It was pleasant to Adrian that the jolting made Viola creep as it were within his protection. The woman on the other side of him might have been a stuffed sack. He had a peculiar excitement in his chest, not unlike terror. We are going up into the barrier, he said to himself; and God knows what will become of my thoughts.

After a while the road relaxed in severity and they descended into the valley where the Sinclair's farm was, a valley watered by a torrent that came down from the iron heart of the mountains with troops of weeping willow and golden poplar. The Sinclair's house was built on a rock by a stream, not very high; and Adrian, looking out of the window, could see a fine rainbow trout. The man Ross quickly put together his rod and angled for the fish, with success.

It clouded over and there were showers, up here in the mountains. These were the clouds Adrian so often watched from the hot plain. Most of the party spent the afternoon fishing; but Viola wanted to show Adrian the neighbourhood. After lunch, therefore, she took him walking, and they explored the stream. 'To-morrow we shall get horses and ride into the mountains,' she said. 'We shall meet this river again further up. It leaps down from pool to pool, and it's cold and frightening.'

'Are we to go fishing then?'

'Yes, Adrian. Not for the first time. '

He could hardly bear to hear her say that. She pushed at an old stuck door that creaked and resisted. It gave him pleasure to watch her, to reflect that if he liked he could take and kiss her.

They were crossing the river on stepping stones. When she gave him her hand he could draw her close, here on this rock in the rushing stream under weeping willows. But he still waited. And why did he experience a restlessness that would not let him stay one moment to gaze at anything beautiful?

They came back to the village, that sad lost village among the mountains, about seven o'clock. Viola leaned on the wooden parapet of the bridge. Downstream, the valley opened out a little between woods and high turfy downs; the house squatted on its rock about a hundred yards off.

'I feel as if the world had altered in some way,' she said. 'As if I were here for the first time.'

'It's very wonderful and melancholy,' Adrian said.

'Melancholy?'

'Yes. Look at that!' He turned round and pointed. The weeping-willows and dimmed golden poplars trooped upward into the stark mountains; high over the gorge where they disappeared towered sharp crags, remote, grey with evening. 'It's a procession going up to some terrible cold place,' he said. 'They die there, the trees.' Viola listened with troubled eyes. 'I feel as if I ought to go with them,' he said, 'and spend my life in the mountains.'

'I believe life holds just that for me.' Viola spoke in slow, sad tones. 'I am to do nothing but go up into high, cold places.' She drooped, and put out a hand towards Adrian. But suddenly, as if a shroud were snatched off them, the crags shone crimson;

a golden light spread over the whole aspect of the mountains; the ascending trees were touched with new fire. Viola's eyes lit too. 'Have you ever seen the world change like that?' she cried.

'Yes. It's the last thing before twilight.' He laughed. 'I'm sentimental. I want a drink.' He made her go into the inn by the bridge. It was necessary for him to put down two or three gin-sours, because of a certain nameless misery that had no horizon. For further protection, when they sat at the table by the window, he drew a little close to her; they leaned together, watching a boy in high-heeled boots and monstrous spurs deal with a jibbing horse. It was a spectacle. The villagers lashed the horse with thongs, and its rider kicked it in the face with his blunted spur; the horse revolved, or dashed at the wall, bucked, reared, did everything that a horse can; the rider sat like a gyroscope. Adrian and Viola watched the scene as if it had no cruelty, no meaning. With a shower of sparks, horse and rider set off full gallop; the two sat and stared at the empty road. 'Better go now,' said Adrian.

The whole party joined in a game of poker-patience after dinner. Adrian played with a zest that he felt to be hectic.

[- 3 -]

NEXT morning, after breakfast, they set off for a fishing expedition in the mountains. It was a hot day with a good deal of cloud. Horses with sheep-skin saddles were waiting for them under the trees in the village. Adrian was surprised when Sinclair, leading, rode straight up the opposite bank and vanished into the bushes. He followed, in his turn, wondering if he would manage to keep his feet in the shallow, shovel-shaped stirrups. He found himself one of a line of horsemen clambering up and down a stony path between bushes. The procession wound along valleys filled with the weeping-willow and golden poplar that marked the stream's course. They went sliding down mud-shoots, burst their way through rivers and pushed deep into thickets from which the horses alone knew the way out. All the time, in spite of several precipitous descents when the path led through some rushing, rock-broken river, they mounted into wilder regions with no growth but spiny bushes, and rode under the gaze of summits. At this stage the horses took possession. One minute Adrian was stretched over the neck, the next gazing down between his heels at some glade or watercourse in a valley. 'I feel like a cinema-star,' he said to Ross as they rubbed knees through a boulder-strewn passage.

293

'Leave it to the horse,' Ross replied. 'They climb like cats.'

Adrian left it to the horse; he prayed to the horse when they rode for a quarter of a mile on a broken path with a long roll of a thousand feet to the valley, and not a tree stump to catch them. Viola turned round and smiled. 'You look solemn,' she said. Adrian smiled back. He felt empty this morning; ready for something to flow in and take possession. It should be Viola. He pressed after her when the path broadened.

After two hours' riding they were in a stupendous hollow of the mountains, going among spiny bushes towards a cleft through which the torrent poured. Walls of rock rose out of seas of scrub and heather all round them; cloud and rain drifted on the high edges of the hollow; snow-peaks showed beyond the cleft. The trees looked small; Adrian felt small on his horse.

They fetched a circle at the head of the basin, drew rein, dismounted and unsaddled among aromatic bushes and trees at the edge of a gorge. Adrian made his way through the bushes and looked over. The river flowed far below, noiseless, a driblet, hardly big enough to hold fish. Opposite rose three thousand feet of rock, with two strata worked by the hand of time into the semblance of bas-reliefs by some gigantic and quite untrammelled sculptor, a colossal rhythm of torsos, thighs, breasts and the stark parts of the body.

Presently came Sinclair. 'Are you ready?'

'Yes.'

'We go down there.'

'We've got to work hard for our fishing.'

Sinclair smiled. 'We assemble here about two o'clock for lunch.' Adrian began to go down with the others, sliding on loose earth, clinging by precarious roots, giving someone a shoulder. The stream was no driblet after all, but a torrent of snow-water that boomed from pool to pool in a thick stream, drowning all other voices. It was hard even to gain access to the pools, for what had looked like small stones from the top proved to be huge boulders, and there was a dense growth of some spiny plant and some plant with prickly burrs that found their way to the skin. On the other side of the torrent the mountain rose treeless, perpendicular. Adrian felt tinier than ever, exerting himself fantastically at the base of that unclimbable wall. Indeed, he felt distinctly oppressed down here, small and alien, as if the mountains did not know him and he had no longer any place in the affection of high and invisible beings. Up there through the cleft a sharp peak of snow looked afar, making no account of minute Adrian. He really began to feel it as a relief that he was insignificant. Adrian put together his rod, and the sensation that he dissolved and became nothing was now altogether delicious, because with it he escaped responsibility. The members of the party had separated, each choosing his pool. There was no sign of any human being except Viola, who stayed with him as if they had come expressly to be together.

'We use worms here,' she said.

They stood side by side baiting their hooks. Adrian could think of nothing to say.

'We've done quite well here with worms,' she said.

Lightly, and as if without meaning to, he kissed her soft, flushed cheek. They separated, going each to an appointed ledge, and Viola's very silence was a promise. They moved on from pool to pool, and patiently caught nothing for about two hours. The noise of the waterfalls made conversation impossible. 'I'm beginning to be fed up,' Adrian said, passing her. 'This kind of fishing is not contemplative. Not that I want to contemplate, at the moment.' She answered his look, but she didn't know all there was in his meaning. He went on to the next pool and lost sight of her. To reach a point where he could fish the pool, a wide, black and swirling pool with a steep thunderous fall on the far side, it became necessary to pass by a narrow ledge. He went several yards; then, holding on to a crack overhead with one hand and carrying his rod in the other, he paused. Better wait here and warn Viola to go round. He turned to see if she was coming: his feet slid and he fell in.

A queer situation, he thought. He had caught the ledge with his right hand, but there was no hold for his feet and he could not pull himself up on to that narrow ledge or do more than keep head and shoulders above water. I must try and not lose the rod, he thought. He managed to dispose of it neatly on the edge, and considered his position.

Better call out, he thought, and yelled 'Viola!' though she would never have heard, and there was no place where she could stand and help him. The water was icy, and it began to be difficult to retain his hold with numbed hands. From this level the pool looked wide as a sea, black and deadly; there was no top to that wall opposite. The only thing was to kick off and let the stream carry him; one would surely be able to catch one of those rocks before being swept into the rapids. He contemplated the smooth sliding edge where the stream discharged itself in a torrent, and was reluctant to give himself to the cold will of that mountain-water. I might actually be drowned here, he thought. Why not? An answer to all problems. There was a moment when he considered this as one outside of himself; a moment followed by most natural panic. Viola did not come, and the cold was paralysing his fingers. There was nothing for it but to let the water decide. He abandoned his own will in the matter and let go. Much else went in that abandonment: he had an experience of infinite relief, an experience like joy. In a few moments, bleeding and exhilarated, he found himself clinging to a rock with both hands while his feet were swept downwards in the torrent. The position was worse than before; but it was easy for Viola, who, when she saw him, had the sense to go round. It was a long time while she made her way through boulders and undergrowth; but the certainty of destruction if he let go now gave a

kind of warmth to his fingers and he hung on. I
suppose a worm feels like this on the end of a line,
he thought. Viola is bound to appear in a minute.
Perhaps she won't be in time. Now he was without
wish to die. Good; there she came creeping over the
rocks. Presently, well planted between two boulders,
she held out the butt of her rod. With the aid of
her rod he manœuvred himself towards her, and
then, taking her hand, climbed out. 'Stupid,' he
said. 'I was in a bit of a panic.' But what he
remembered more than the panic, and still experienced, was the luxury of that act of abandonment.
'One always feels gay after danger, if there was
danger,' he said. 'One wants to talk.'

But Viola wouldn't listen. 'You go straight up
to the. top,' she said, 'and get into dry clothes. .
You've got spare things?'

'Yes. But I shall be hot and dry enough by the
time I get up there.' He glanced at the fringe of
aromatic bushes and trees that looked over the
gorge. 'Look at my watch. I've ruined it, I suppose.
And about four hundred dollars, sopping.' He
still wanted to talk and make jokes.

'Off you go,' Viola said. 'At once. I'm coming as
well.'

Adrian carefully recovered his rod, and took it
to pieces. They began the ascent. After the first
two hundred feet of zigzagging among boulders
and spiny bushes, they took the wrong route and
found themselves faced with slope after slope of
loose soil. They struggled on, kicking and scramb-

ling, holding by root or tree whenever the hold looked secure. Once or twice it gave, and one or the other slipped back a few feet. 'I like that sensation of slipping away into nothing,' Adrian said.

'You look like I don't know what,' Viola replied.

His wet clothes had picked up a skin of dirt; fingers and forehead were still bleeding from the rocks. He was hot, exhausted and exultant. 'I'm enjoying this struggle.'

'I'm.not,' she said. 'I can't do much more. We were stupid to come this way.'

He saw her slender form droop. 'One more effort,' he urged. 'Let's get over to those rocks . . . they look climbable.'

She obeyed. They traversed and found a platform to rest on. But it was a question how to go further. 'About fifty feet to the top,' Adrian said. 'There's only one way.' He pointed it out—twenty feet up a sort of shoot in the rocks; a right-handed traverse across an earth slope to a convenient ledge; an arm's reach to a tree; one pull, and you would be lying in a grassy, green place under bushes at the top of the cliff.

'I can't manage it,' Viola said.

'Well, I've got an idea.' Adrian started ahead.

'No. Don't go. Stay with me.'

'I'll stay with you in that little green place.' He pointed. They would be alone under the aromatic trees. Oh, it would be marvellous to lie beside her, draw her close, taste her, brown, deep-eyed, Viola! Viola was soon lost to sight. After the first scramble up that gully his heart pounded, and the slope looked impossible. But Adrian was occupied with other sensations. He took four or five steps out sideways, and looked . up and down and around, at the line of the cliff overhead, the driblet of water below, a snowpeak away there through the cleft. Shadows like the figures of gods and daemons moved along the huge wall of the gorge, and clouded the bushes down by the torrent, and entangled his feet. He stood still, listening to voices, mountain voices, singing in chorus. It had been unhappy, that isolation of his mind, decreed by some insolence of the will. He felt the earth giving and made a gesture, as if throwing everything to the winds. By some miraculous change, mind and will were taken up again into the self that was at home with these mountains and heard their voices. Adrian went on, moving as if he suffered, amazed like one long dead who emerges from darkness into the living world, still tortured by the unfreezing of the blood. Presently he reached out a hand and pulled himself into the green dell. He made a way through the bushes to the place where the horses were tied up, took the lasso from his saddle, and returned, trembling for some unknown cause, to the spot that he judged to be just over Viola's head. Yes, there she was. There was no difficulty when she had tied herself on the rope. Adrian helped her up the rocks and across the slope and into the dell. There she fell into the grass, where he enfolded her and kissed her

300

many times. But he desisted presently with a kind of shame; for he perceived in her stony face that she knew from his relaxing hands and sudden weeping that he longed for somebody else.

[- 4 -]

FOR the next few hours, the necessity of engaging with Viola kept Adrian's resurgent feelings in bounds. Her behaviour was wonderful. She showed no more during lunch than what might be taken for a trace of weariness. After lunch Adrian said he wouldn't fish any more. 'I got rather chilled, he said, 'and I don't want to do any more climbing. I shall ride home.'

'I'll come too, and show you the way,' Viola said, accepting his glance. She appeared calm. Within himself, he was suppressing exultation. For the present he must accept Viola's grief.

They saddled and rode off by a new path, wilder and more startling than the path they had come by. But Adrian didn't notice it at the time. Viola led. First they cantered down grassy slopes among trees, and came after a mile or so to the torrent, where two of the party were fishing. They crossed a tributary stream, and Adrian's beast stopped to drink: he looked down its long neck at the stones in the running water. They had a view now of mountains ahead, with shadows of clouds on them. Somewhere in that wilderness of huge shapes was their own village, and the farm where last night they had been merry enough. Adrian kicked the broad belly of his horse, and pressed on after Viola, who was going hard. He hadn't seen her face since they started. It was necessary to speak. 'Viola . . . I can't say anything that doesn't sound horrible. . . .'

She turned her face. 'Obviously you can't. There's only one thing I want to hear in the world . . . you know it . . . I don't mind saying it. But I've always known you were given to Linet like a sort of doom.' She spoke so quietly. The horses were up to their bellies in a river; Adrian felt the cold water steal into his boot. Viola wheeled and faced him. 'I don't know what's been happening to you — you wouldn't tell me. But you've been far away all the time you were with us, even when you imagined you wanted me. You were dead. Something has happened in your mind now?'

'Yes. Now as once before; but more startling.'

'You know beyond doubt that you are in love with Linet.'

'That and much more.' He was going to say: Don't ask me, my feelings will be unbearable if you wake them; but it seemed best to say least. Without meaning to he jerked at the horse's mouth. They scrambled out of the river, and up a steep path between trees, where it was necessary to duck and swerve. Viola followed hard. The cloud shadows pursued them and passed them and swept onwards over the mountains.

Now they must cross a barren slope of the mountain by a narrow path. Her voice came after him in its familiar, soft, modulations. 'You two seem to be hopeless without each other,' she said.

303

'You actually experience the same things at the same time. It's true marriage. I don't know why I never accepted my own knowledge.' There was a pause. 'She will be waiting for you — Oh yes!' A long silence; then, 'You will do windows again?'

'Why, yes. Marvellous windows!'

He turned in his saddle to see her. She smiled a little. What were her secret thoughts as she followed along the high windy path on a slope of the mountain? Ahead, the path ended apparently in a view. How Linet would enjoy this! It was wrong to exult, in company with this sad lovely girl; but there was a passion in Adrian's chest that would not be eased without strong action. His heart cried out: Linet! I'll ride by peak and cloud; I'll kick down the Andes to reach you!

But the horse chose its own pace, and it was hard, for with the utterance of that name there nearly went out his soul. They came to a platform from which the path went down steeply, and Viola was beside him. 'At the end of this path,' she said, 'there will be nothing. While we are still here there is something. I don't seem to mind telling you. . . .'

Adrian wheeled, leant over her saddle and drew her close. 'Oh Viola! If I had loved anyone else it would have been you. I do love you. God forgive me . . . I bring nothing but trouble into people's lives. . . .'

'No, love does that. It'll go on for you till you've paid. As for me I shall pay with loneliness and weeping.'

Adrian scarcely understood at the time; just now he was too sad with her sadness to enquire into strange meanings. 'There's been at any rate this special thing between us,' he began . . . but what use was it? What could he say that wasn't just out of place?

Viola replied to his thoughts. 'Don't let's say any more.' She looked long in his face with passionate eyelids. 'Except this: I wish I'd had you before this change.'

Adrian hid his face in her cheek. 'Don't answer,' she said, and pulled her horse round with a jerk and set off. Adrian followed, and grief for her grief kept him, for the time being, from his own. This lasted when the ride was over, and they dismounted and stood for a minute on the bridge, looking back at the crags whose crimson flare was glory for Adrian and grief for Viola. It lasted throughout the evening, when they were all back in the farm, playing cards. Adrian could do nothing but watch her, and pay tribute to her admirable behaviour. It lasted through the night when he was awake with her thoughts. It ended next day, when they returned to Santiago, and he said good-bye.

In the hotel at Valparaiso Adrian took a big bare room with white walls, black floorboards and doors, and a white net curtain in the window. There was no ship for some days, and in any case he wanted to test himself against his emotions, this throng of longings, doubts, jealousies that clamoured at the doors of his mind. He sat in his room, or walked the streets, or stared at the ships and the cold Pacific, and strange thoughts presented themselves, with the shape of malignant beings. You've lost her, said one. She will have been unfaithful, with faith lost. Tracy . . . He heard names. She will have used degradation as a medicine, a voice suggested. If you re-engage with her it will come to the same thing over again. The end will be madness, suicide, murder.

The end will be nothing of the sort, Adrian argued. You don't understand there has been a change that makes everything different, and renders the future possible. You don't understand anything. You don't know of the death of a whole part of me: that is, your own death. He looked. Yes, these passions were white-faced, lacking in vitality, depotentialized. He felt confidence. As to Linet, I don't know exactly what will have been the order of her experiences; but her soul lives and changes with mine. I shall expose your arguments by

306

means of a telegram. He wrote out a telegram at the hall-porter's desk. 'I want you: Adrian.' That night it was certainly a struggle to keep his anxieties at bay. The answer came next afternoon. 'You shall have me then: Linet.' Adrian waved the telegram in the face of his thoughts: it might be enough to disperse them. They retired at any rate to a distance, leaving him to speculate on the state of her mind towards him.

Having appointed by telegraph to meet Linet in Havana, Adrian took ship, when he could get a berth.

During the voyage Adrian hardly spoke to a soul. The ship was not very full, and he was lucky enough to get a single-berth cabin as well as a table to himself. Morning and afternoon he took exercise at deck-tennis with the captain and swam in the canvas tank; all the rest of the day he spent by himself, drawing in his cabin, strolling from end to end of the ship, or sitting alone on the boat-deck where he could stare at the mountainous coast, the smug pelicans fantastically sailing past, the por-poises, and the seals that poked their brown heads sideways out of the sea. It was halcyon weather. He found the rhythmical roll and plunge of the ship conducive to patience and meditation; the unfolding of that iron, inhospitable coast, the panorama of high peaks and majestic cloud, gave a solemn tinge to his thoughts; he was calm and joyous, and one afternoon, when they were out of sight of land and there was nothing to be seen except stretches of the Pacific fading into sadness, he stood outside his own life, and nothing in the world had power to affect him, not even his love. It was deep happiness. And even during the experience he knew that he would never have it again. Life would recover some of its power over him, and he would know grief.

At first his thoughts circled like the sea-birds with never-ending changes of rhythm. His own past was before him, exhibiting itself in a kind of accidental pattern of no beauty. It seemed as if the man he now was had emerged from a mist and welter, with dawn-glories in it and a sort of murk. To begin with, there was indetermination, tendencies beginning and ending, purposes dissolved in cross-currents of the mind, a vague consciousness, a passionate identification of the self with people and things. How long, for instance, before he conceived of a work of art as something possessing unity? Until so lately he merely took pleasure in separate parts that came brilliantly, in disconnected colour, in spontaneous but unrelated execution, in the representation of exterior things passionately and confusedly felt. Then, succumbing to malady, frightened for some reason of certain real elements and superior partners in his own soul, he annihilated genius in the study of form. And how long until he conceived of love as an art requiring concentration, the management of forces into one channel, a technique far more difficult than he practised in glass? It must have been in him to know this; for he recognized Linet that she was for him the embodiment of all that is delightful to the senses and to the spirit, and his feeling for life all flowed to the one point at the sight of her. Through what misadventure did he come so near to throwing all this away? The double insanity arose from the same cause, an attempt to escape from the power of life without paying his debts, to escape indeed to the region where he now was and did not passionately wish to remain. Adrian rose from his chair without knowing that he did so, and went to the rail, and stood staring out westward where the sun lowered in splendour towards extinction. There were thoughts at present beyond Adrian's grasp or expression, glimpses of high peaks and cloudless wells in the sky. He knew himself as part of a wider consciousness, like a flaw in glass. Some day the knot might resolve. But now, he said, now to the paying of debts, to loving and creating. I will acknowledge the things of which I am part, that create by means of me; whatever I create shall be their work, subject only to due criticism of the mind. There will be union of life with pattern. And as to Linet, I will no longer withhold myself through self-regard, put forward in the form of some nonsense about giving myself to art. She shall have me, so that her nature and the life of her soul may flourish! And as to God! Adrian smiled to think that he had sought after God with his intellect, expecting answers. God is to be known as an activity of the human soul, he said; and

I know Him. God and the Devil are aspects of the same thing. And one day, when my time comes, I shall be delivered from both. But that is not now. Now I must give myself to life. Life, however, that will have much less power over me.

Adrian looked to the future. I accept life, he said, as experience shows it to be, including my passion for Linet: I offer life no clothes. He began to return into his altered self and consider the art of living. Those two main and autonomous principles that had established themselves in the welter of indetermination — a spontaneous creative power, a necessity for the body and friendship of a woman prefigured in his mind and senses — belonged in some way to one another and must be lived out. There would be difficulties! But at least there was no longer any malignancy. Surely those evils were outgrown. In future there should be no use of the will, except to set going the soul's power of superseding itself . . . Having this secret it should be simple to cope with things, delightful, a work worth doing! I shall be able to finish Pollock's windows. Adrian stretched out his arms, gigantic for Linet, vital with a life and power that was more than himself.

[- 6 -]

ADRIAN was definitely relieved when the ship emerged on the Atlantic side of the Panama Canal. This world was familiar; the Pacific world, alien, teeming, contained oppressive recollections. After a steamy hot evening in Colon the ship headed once more for the open sea, and a breeze blew. Adrian, in his new relief and affability, spoke to the man beside him. 'How cruel our egoism is!' he observed.

'I don't precisely get your connection, sir.'

'It doesn't matter, sir. I shouldn't have been talking aloud.'

'I agree with your sentiment,' the other man said, 'and I should like to enjoy your conversation. My name is Root, sir, Julius Root.'

'Mine's Adrian Douglas.'

Julius Root, one of those idiosyncratic, judicious men, like Huxtable and Pollock, who presided in succession over his destiny, perused Adrian's sun-beaten, mahogany face. 'You certainly are *the* Mr. Adrian Douglas,' he said.

'Why, we haven't met, have we?'

'Have we met? No, sir. It's this way. I'm a theosophist, Mr. Douglas. There's something in that religion just corresponds with my way of look-ing at things. Well, I once saw windows of yours in New York, and when I was in London on my way back from India — yes, sir, I've got interests in most

311

parts of this world, as well as in the next — they showed me your big window in our church there. It's a great window, Mr. Douglas. I was interested, and I enquired where I could see some more. Well, it was fixed up for me, and I went around and I arrived at the conclusion that you are a considerable artist, and I'm glad to meet you.'

Adrian wriggled and tried to turn the conversation; but Mr. Root was not to be put off. 'I made a short trip to Barcelona,' he said, 'and there's a Madonna in a kind of chapel there got right under my skin.'

'That's my wife,' Adrian said.

'Is that so?'

'Yes, I did that window before ever I saw her.'

'Is that so? Well, if that doesn't show there's things we don't understand.'

'I'm meeting her in Havana,' Adrian said.

'Well, Mr. Douglas, if that isn't just fortunate! It happens my agent's taken a little place for me right there in the suburbs. I'll be happy to put it at your disposal.'

Adrian thanked him. Next morning they spent a couple of hours talking; and at the end of their conversation he definitely accepted the offer, with other things. It was a bright, buoyant day, the sea an intense light blue with silver cloud-reflections, and one great white castle of a cloud making a silver cloud-road. They sat on the upper deck watching the flying-fish that scattered from the ship's path.

'I've got a little shooting-box near Washington,' Mr. Root said, 'on the Patuxent, and I'm just crazy on ducks. I've got some Chinese pictures there, Mr. Douglas, that'll interest you quite a lot. I'd like to have you do three or four little windows for my study there. I want you to do for America what the unknown painter did for the Sung Dynasty. I want you to create a duck, in glass.'

'I'd be glad to try,' Adrian said.

'And I'm building myself a home in Florida, Mr. Douglas, quite a mansion, with a little church. I'd be glad to have you advise me on that.'

'It would give me great pleasure. It happens I'm full of ideas.'

'I congratulate myself that I came home way round by South America,' Mr. Root said. 'Yes, I've got interests in those Republics. I've been meditating a lot since I saw your glass, Mr. Douglas. I'd thought of a new kind of conservatory . . .' The American outlined his ideas. Adrian, fired, gave them shape and colour. The two days to Havana passed quickly while they built structures of glass. 'How new I am!' Adrian reflected. 'Nothing quite like this has come out of me before. Of course, in the right climate one can see it — a discreet use of opaque glass in patterns, with a decoration of foliage and appropriate scenes. Doors, vestibules, screens, colonnades. A swimming pool. Here's a man rich enough to facilitate new uses . . . Perhaps I'm too excited, because of to-morrow. . . .'

313

Next afternoon they berthed in Havana and Mr.
Root took Adrian straight to an elegant country
house with Chinese servants, and open windows,
and masses of temperate flowers in the garden,
and breezes from the sea. Their conversations
enabled Adrian to get through the two days that,
as he learnt, must pass before Linet's ship was
expected, and the nights in a large summery room
where already he heard her whispering.

Mr. Root was an admirable man who guessed a
lot without asking questions. On the day Linet was
due, he said, 'I've got to go right off to Manzanillo
on the other side of the island. I've got some plan-
tations there. I'll be glad for you to stay here with
Mrs. Douglas and do just what you like.' He departed, and Adrian went down to the docks. There
was Linet's ship in the river, turning round. It
seemed hours while the great steamer moved
tidally to the appointed place, and long before
they made fast Adrian saw Linet, standing by the
rail in new clothes like a stranger, very small and
still. They made scarcely any sign to each other,
as if they dared not acknowledge their own secret.
There was Anthony bobbing up and down in charge
of a nurse and shouting. Adrian waved to the child,
but he looked only at Linet, and searched for indica-
tions of the state of her mind towards him. She
gave none. And when she came out of the ship's
side and down the gangway and he kissed her it
was like kissing a stranger. It was a stranger who
rode with him in the car. She said, 'A little like

Brighton, only hot and with palm trees,' and looked through the window all the six miles along that avenue thick with tobacco plant that came out at evening, all colours. Adrian took Anthony on his knee, and the new nurse stole glances at him. Even when he took Linet up to their summery bedroom and showed her the gardens and paddocks and the view of green country with glimpses of blue Caribbean, even when he put his arms round her, she was absent, though responding. Oh, but he knew the scent and taste of her and longed for her to come back! It was certainly the shape and habit of Linet that went straight to the white bathroom, through those high, theatrical doors, and turned on the silver taps and undressed, saying, 'I'm simply filthy;' but she remained impersonal. At dinner, with two Chinese servants to wait on them, he kept glancing at the radiant person in the green frock to see if it was really Linet. Yes, for she had chosen the green frock to please him, and the style of her conversation was familiar. There were familiar names. 'Gwatkin was funny about the money to come here with,' she said. 'He grudged it. I hated asking because . . . yes . . . because Gwatkin was a nuisance.' This she said to Adrian's enquiring eyebrow. 'He seemed to lose hold of something when you left. He went over to Tracy's side of the argument; much further. He rather disgusted me. Tracy could never do that.' Adrian inspected his plate. 'Mark was the only one who gave no trouble at all,' she said. 'And he was so kind, especially when Tracy went too. Yes, Tracy took himself off. I can only tell you that I found out something about myself.' She laughed. 'Your face always comes up when I look at another man.' She caught his eye between the electric candles and glanced away. This was my own experience, he thought. But was it as welcome with her? Or did she regret it?

Better indicate the style of his own history. 'I had the same experience,' he told her. They might have been strangers talking about rhinoceros hunting. 'There'll be no bother about money,' he added. 'Mark telegraphs there's plenty to do, and I've got something as well. Rather promising, if practicable.' He told her about Julius Root.

She listened. 'It'll be fun to be in America again,' she said. 'I went to New York with Carl once.' Adrian was happy to find that this statement had no power over him. But he was puzzled, for in her conversation and demeanour she seemed to accept everything, yet remained unknowable. It was a stranger who stood with him afterwards in the paddock, under an apple tree, and answered his kisses; a stranger who undressed in the high, night-perfumed room and came willingly to bed with him. 'You shall have me, then,' she had said in her telegram. He was calm, having patience to conjure her from the dead. How still she lay in her silk shroud!

'I'm confused,' he said, gazing back at the spirit face that gazed at him from the moon-flooded pillows. 'You are Linet?'

'Yes, and you are Adrian.'

'It's difficult to believe that we're together, in this island.'

A smile crossed her face. 'We make love best in strange places.'

He considered. 'I shall never take you back to that house.'

'Why? I don't mind.' She laid her cheek on the pillow and looked into the dark spaces of the room. 'I've got over that. The house has no power over me.'

Thoughts streamed through his mind. 'I'm not the same as I was,' he told her, after a while.

'Nor I.'

'I've climbed a little way out of myself.'

'I, too. Yes, I can see you are changed, Adrian. It's in your face, in your manner. As in mine, no doubt.'

'If I went back to that house,' he insisted, 'it would be like giving myself to old dark passions. They may get me anyway.'

She turned her face again and her eyes looked past him at moonlight and flowers in the window. 'They may get us both,' she admitted. 'But since this change in myself I'm not afraid of them.'

'You feel that? As if those daemons have been devitalized?'

'Yes; when we quarrel next we shall be detached from our feelings. I can't explain . . . anger won't be so real.' She crossed her fingers and touched the wooden bedpost.

317

'And love?'

'Not so real either.'

He left the bed and stood a little while by the window, plucking leaves. After meditation he returned to the bed with some petals and laid them on her.

'I wonder if "real" is the word,' he said presently. 'You mean we've destroyed the malignant power that there is in love by understanding it?'

'I hope so.'

'Leaving us the better part, that marvel, that heavenly knowledge?'

'I think so.'

'We shall enjoy a certain lightness or transparency of being,' he said. 'We shall enter each other's personality without stirring up clouds.' He strove to express a truth recently possessed in timeless contemplation. 'There's blessedness in release from pleasure as well as from pain . . . but oh, Linet! my chastened heart still beats!'

'Mine too. Indeed Adrian.'

'I have to win you again,' he whispered.

'You have my heart, now and for ever.'

'Is it faith makes you give yourself?'

'Yes, for we're not angels. That's why I'm in bed with you. We have to live in the world, and for that we must look to what's happened. How can we do other than believe in our own experience that we've both had, and follow it?'

He could still hardly believe that it was Linet's voice whispering so close to him. He put his cheek

on the pillow beside her. This was the lobe of her
ear, this her knee, this her breast. 'I can feel the
heart beat under your rabbit ribs,' he said, and
she smiled to hear him use a familiar endearment.

'We've only had a little bit of our lives,' she said,
'and we haven't paid everything yet.' She turned
to him. They became grave, looking in each other's
dark, gazing eyes; grave and tense.

'What do you see?' he asked.

'Windows. Your work will be full of new things
and that strange meaning that is You. I'm glad.
Oh, I'm glad to see you looking down at me again,
and I'm not frightened like I used to be.' She lifted
her mouth close to his. 'What do you see in me,
staring so deep?'

'A little fair girl with long legs and big eyes and
hair blowing like gossamer.'

'Adrian! that poor Selena! She'll have so many
strange things in her!' It was Linet who slipped from
the silk shroud.

CPSIA information can be obtained at www.ICGtesting.com
Printed in the USA
BVOW01s0004130315

391543BV00015B/120/P